Fully Sikh

Sukhjit Kaur Khalsa

Sukhjit Kaur Khalsa is a writer, performer, theatre-maker, filmmaker, and producer based in Boorloo. Her work as a multi-form artist for the last ten years has been recognised at the Performing Arts WA Awards (2020), Mona Brand Writing Awards (2022), WA Multicultural Awards (2022) and Young Australian Sikh of the Year (2023). Her passion for storytelling began as a finalist in the Australian Poetry Slam (2014), semi-finalist on *Australia's Got Talent* (2016) and winner of The Moth Grand Slam (2019).

Sukhjit premiered her sell-out theatre work *Fully Sikh* with Barking Gecko Theatre Company and Black Swan Theatre Company (2019). Since then, she has been developing her comedy series *What Would Suki Do?* with support from ABC TV, and is currently producing *A Hairy Tale*, a documentary exploring female body hair. Sukhjit presented at Tedx UWA (2017), Tedx Newtown (2019) and has supported Missy Higgins and L-Fresh the Lion on their national tours. Her poetry and community arts projects have led her to tour globally and across her nation.

Sukhjit and her partner, Perun Bonser, were selected to develop their rom-com series *One of the Good Ones* at Ron Howard & Brian Grazer's talent lab, Impact Australia (2020). They premiered their video installation work *Between Breaths* at Goolugatup Heathcote Art Gallery (2022), and the work toured in 4A Contemporary Asian Art Centre's Bush Diwan (2022–23). Sukhjit worked as a story-telling trainer at the Centre for Stories and has produced storytelling and theatre projects for adults and school students. Collectables, her debut hip-hop single, is now streaming on all platforms.

Sukhjit is currently the Executive Director of The Blue Room Theatre in Perth/Boorloo.

Sukhjit Kaur Khalsa

Fully Sikh

hot chips and turmeric stains

First published in Australia in 2025
by Upswell Publishing
Perth, Western Australia
upswellpublishing.com

Upswell operates in the city of Perth, on ancient country of the Whadjuk people of the Noongar nation who remain the spiritual and cultural custodians of this beautiful land. We acknowledge their continuing connection to country and express gratitude to elders past and present for their strength and creativity...Always was, always will be, Aboriginal land.

ISBN: 978-0-6459840-6-4

A catalogue record for this
book is available from the
National Library of Australia

Cover design by Chil3, Fremantle
Typeset in Foundry Origin by Lasertype
Printed by McPherson's Printing Group

Upswell Publishing is assisted by the State of Western Australia through its funding program for arts and culture.

ਮੈਂ ਇਸ ਧਰਤੀ ਦੇ Traditional Owners ਮਤਲਬ Noongar ਕੌਮ ਤੋ ਇਜਾਜ਼ਤ ਮੰਗਣਾ ਚਾਹੂੰਗੀ ਅਪਣੀ ਕਹਾਣੀ ਸੱਬ ਨੂੰ ਦਸੱਣ ਲਈ।

ਮੈਂ ਇੱਕ ਗਲ ਦੀ ਕਦਰ ਕਰਨਾ ਚਾਉਂਦੀ ਹਾਂ। ਪੰਤਾਲੀ ਹਜ਼ਾਰ ਸਾਲ ਤੋ ਉਹਨਾ ਨੇ ਅੱਪਣੀ ਰਾਜਸੱਤਾ ਨੂੰ ਪੂਰਵਜਾਂ ਦੀਆਂ ਕਹਾਣਿਆ ਸੁੱਣਾ ਕੇ ਅੱਤੇ ਕਲਾ ਨਾਲ ਜਿਉਂਦਾ ਰਖਿਆ ਹੈ।

ਸਾਡੇ ਗੁਰੂ ਸਾਹੇਬਾਨ ਨੇ ਸਾਰੀ ਜ਼ਿਦਗੀ ਮਨੁੱਖੀ ਹੱਕਾਂ ਦੀ ਰਖਿਆ ਕਰਨਾ ਸਿਖਾਇਆ। ਇਸੇ ਕਰਕੇ ਇੱਕ ਸਿੱਖ ਹੋਣ ਦੇ ਨਾਤੇ ਮੈਂ ਸੌਂ ਚੁੱਕਦੀ ਹਾਂ ਕਿ ਮੈਂ ਪੂਰੀ ਕੋਸ਼ਸ਼ ਨਾਲ First Nations ਨੂੰ ਸਮਰਥਨ ਕਰਦੀ ਹਾਂ ਅੱਤੇ ਕਰਦੀ ਰਹੂੰਗੀ।

ਇਹ Aboriginal-ਆਂ ਦੀ ਧਰਤੀ ਹੈ ਤੇ ਸਦਾ ਹੀ ਰਹੇਗੀ।

Translation:

I would like to seek permission from the Traditional Owners of this land, the Noongar people, to share my story.

I wish to acknowledge there is a long line of resilience, storytelling and art that existed over 45,000 years ago and sovereignty has never been ceded.

My Gurus spent their lives inspiring others to stand up for human rights and equality, so as a Sikh I would like to pledge my commitment to support First Nations people.

Always was, always will be, Aboriginal land.

Author's Note

The writings in *Fully Sikh* range across a vast landscape of the author's life – all the way from primary school to the current time.

Our [Sikh] history is of the soul; all its events are of the soul. All truth for us is personal. We have not to prove it, we have to stand witness to it in our soul . . . Rise and fill yourselves with this glory. It makes you noble, bold and free, self-drunk, selfless, flower-like, sun-like . . . Perpetual spring must roll in you. You shall be the moral influence radiating peace, goodwill, friendship, fellowship, life, vigour, vitality, in short, spirituality.

Professor Puran Singh, 1928

Contents

Gurdwara Day

We're celebrating my nephew's third birthday at Kwinana Adventure Park. It's the most multicultural park I've ever been to in Perth. I see a Noongar toddler racing with my niece on the flying fox, I hear Afro beats from a Nigerian family's picnic, and Mum passes out pizza slices in our Punjabi version of *Modern Family*. I know this might sound like a clichéd 'I am, you are, we are Australian' campaign, but the moment catches me off guard. It's unusual to not feel like a minority in my own home town. To not feel so alone. Unwanted. An outcast. The Perth I grew up in boasted big backyards and bigotry. Wide skies and high-school bullies. Sacred sunsets and racist policies. Not this utopian UN fantasy!

Let me take you back to when I was born, in May 1994. Apparently, one of the most destructive storms hit the suburbs of Perth the night before my birth, leaving one-third of the city in darkness. I like to think of it as Mother Nature throwing me a baby shower, welcoming me into the bosom of her universe. My family, on the other hand, saw it as a warning to the citizens of Western Australia that a wild being was about to thunder into their world. Clearly, Waheguru Ji had blessed my parents with a shit-stirrer. Much like Sabrina the Teenage Witch, I only discovered my 'powers' in my late teens. Before that, I was a good little Sikh girl. I did my prayers, obeyed the rules and drank my mandatory glass of warm milk before bed (despite obvious signs of lactose intolerance . . . Mum!).

My cocoon of comfort could be found in two casas: my family home, in Leeming, and my second home, the Gurdwara – our place of worship – in Bayswater. Those walls protected me from internalising white supremacy (and from running away with a non-Sikh bae). At home, I was constantly seeking attention from my older siblings, Manjit and Harjit. I came into the world seven and eight years after them, so naturally we had a pseudo sibling–parent relationship. Not understanding that my sister's teenage dream wasn't to share a bunk bed with a drooling preteen, I'd yank Manjit's yoga pants to play SpongeBob Monopoly or to pretend to be check-out chicks in the walk-in pantry. Even though I'd be interrupting her Year 12 study, she'd always give in and keep me entertained with true big-sis love. My brother was a little harder to convince, but those moments riding our bikes down Westminster Road, smashing out a game of badminton at the rec centre and playing *Crash Bandicoot* were priceless. I looked up to Harjit and at times even wanted to be him. His confidence, charisma and overall coolness were contagious.

On Sundays we would wash our long black manes before packing into the Tarago for the longest religious ritual of all: Gurdwara day. As I sat cross-legged in the back seat, we drove along the Graham Farmer Freeway and into the only tunnel I knew back then. The kirtan (Sikh hymns) blasting from the cassette player would hiss and sizzle with static before we arrived in the northern suburb of Bayswater. I would see the Nishan Sahib, the Sikh flag, reflected in my sister's rimless sunnies (which she'd later get in trouble for wearing inside the Gurdwara) as we pulled up in front of a dark brown, double-bricked former church building. We'd pile out of the Tarago, bumping into familiar families, greeting each other with glee. Cheeks were pinched, perfume was inhaled, and I'd find myself enveloped in folds of fabric and fat.

The Gurdwara was not only a holy sanctuary of cleansing and prayer, but also a social place to gather and chatter. My dad and his bestie would go on long strolls down Murray Street, saluting the sun with their bellies as they digested their ma di dal, two rotis and achaar. Discussing their next committee move, the future of Sikhi, and how they'd run the Gurdwara better than those chumps in charge. Inside,

I'd be learning the history of my ancestors at Punjabi school, the teachings of my Gurus at kirtan class and soaking in what I thought it meant to be Sikh: hairy, harmonious and ultra-compliant.

Gurdwara day also meant that there was a big chance I would get to hang out with my Punjabi besties. Both older and wiser, they had access to accessories I couldn't even dream of: sparkly pink scrunchies to match their chunni (scarves) and watermelon-flavoured Lip Smackers. In the darbar, or prayer hall, we'd catch up on the week's goss in not-so-quiet whispers, try not to snort laugh at our Pinglish jokes and scheme up plans to continue the fun post-prayer. In the langar hall (food hall), we'd already have Operation Playdate in motion. Parents were in perfect positions for our performance of pleading and persuasion. Before they could answer, we'd be belted up in the back seat singing 'Nachna Tere Naal' (a banger by Jay Sean before he became famous).

My Punjabi besties both had the coolest houses: their own bedrooms decorated to teen perfection, multiple entertainment rooms and fancy new trampolines. I wonder if they thought my house was crappy and boring. I shared a room with my sister (and hundreds of soft toys); my dedicated play area was literally inside the wardrobe that connected my parents' bedroom to their bathroom (gross), and our rusty trampoline was an OH&S hazard.

Just when I thought Gurdwara day was over, my family would pick me up from my friend's house and we would take a trip to the latest Indian grocery store, or do fruit picking at our go-to farm in the Perth Hills. And if there was a priest visiting from India, we'd chuck in a scenic tour of Mundaring Dam and end the day boating through the Mandurah canals. (Watch out, Tourism Australia! Khalsa Adventures is here to stay!)

But then I grew into a fully-fledged frustrated teen and everything changed. The tunnel signalled a day of dread that would drag on for way too long. I tried to drown out the kirtan cassettes with my iPod Nano. The carpark pleasantries were far from pleasant. I could barely tolerate a side hug from an uncle or a backhanded compliment from an auntie, and felt more and more distant from my siblings. Gurdwara friendship groups were tumultuous and tense. We grew out of our playdates and instead experimented with our hormone-infused hostility. I hated the stench of the shoe room, where my Havaianas would never last. I hated the creepy toilets, where I'd hear and smell elderly farts. I hated the greasy communal towels. I hated the sweaty, cramped kitchen, where I was forced to roll rotis that never met the standard. I hated walking past uncles with henna-dyed beards, grunting in their plastic chair circles. I hated their head pats. And I hated the sound of little kids playing tag.

I started to see Gurdwara day as a place of judgement, hierarchy, socialising, health problems, enemies, division and politics, and certainly not a place of comfort and spirituality. Those uncles and aunties never seemed to smile with their eyes. They were praying for their children to get good marks, get rich and get married to the right caste. I became more aware of what was really going on in my community. The secrets. The violence. The unhappiness. The expectations. The clashes of culture. The feuds. The wearing down of masculinity. The lack of power. The loneliness. The clinging onto faith. I saw glimpses of intense AGMs. Voices raised. Turbans flying. Vicious words. Swords up. Priests resigning. Women crying into microphones. I think someone even once had to call the police.

I moved to Melbourne after graduating uni. I left my link to spirituality, to Sikhi, and became my own person. I explored who I was outside of the formerly comforting walls of my family and community. My Sikh values were challenged as I navigated adulthood, independence and my career as a performing artist. Through the chaos and calamities of my early twenties, I learnt how to build my own community, work on my own expression of spirituality and cultivate my new-found identity. Rejuvenated and ready, I returned home to Perth stronger, more secure and hungry for the next challenge. And challenged I was.

I fell in love with Perun, a Ngarluma man. Someone outside of my faith and familiar culture. Outside the realms of possibility for a young Sikh woman. I found someone who understood me like no one else did but I took a moment to accept the decision my heart had made. And after a couple of years of confusion and sadness, our relationship was also accepted by my parents. Something I never thought would happen.

After five years together, here we are today at my nephew's third birthday at Kwinana Adventure Park with my modern Punjabi family. My brother with his Sikh Punjabi wife and daughter. My sister with her ex-Muslim Iranian husband and son. And me, shit-stirring with my ex-Catholic Ngarluma partner, childless by choice. Our new Gurdwara days are regularly practised at my parents' house. The grandkids clang along to Dad's kirtan while my sister-in-law and I passionately discuss our next career moves, the future of humanity, and how we'd run the country better than those chumps in charge.

In 2020, I moved to Bayswater with my partner. I started driving through the tunnel on a daily basis. A mundane route that connected me to my family, south of the river. I would get my lactose-free iced latte from the local hipster café, share a margherita pizza at the new bar and smell the rosemary and basil on Slade Street. We survived lockdowns and laparoscopies in Bayswater. I'd never thought I'd be living a couple of streets away from the Gurdwara, my former second home. It was around this time that I started having vivid dreams of taking my partner to the Gurdwara. In my slumber, my partner would appear in different childhood memories, as an auntie with rolls of belly or a henna-bearded uncle or even a giggling Punjabi bestie.

One day, I decided to take him there. I wanted to show him a place that took up a lot of space in my childhood. That informed who I am today. We got dressed in our 'Sunday best' and I nervously arrived at the front of the dark brown, double-bricked former church building. Everything looked smaller and less significant. Less scary. To my surprise, the Nishan Sahib flag had been replaced by a Sai Baba symbol. I saw a Hindu priest hanging out his washing. Same building – different community.

I closed my eyes and imagined the sounds of a Sunday: preteen Hindu kids taking selfies in their hottest outfits, texting their temple friends during prayers, making TikTok videos of their uncles saluting the sun with their bellies, discussing their next committee move, the future of faith, and how they'd run the temple better than those chumps in charge.

To Advance Australia Fair

'If you're not in Australia, where the bloody hell are ya?'
Remember the Bingle jingle?
Inviting the world to mix and mingle?
Where 'a fair go' was your welcome mat,
Unless you're of caramel descent,
Then ain't NObody got tiiiime for dat!

Rockin' up for my first job at Coles,
Was like a scene from Border Patrol.
Her plastic tag read 'Dorothy',
Glasses corded, she hawked, 'Do you have a visa, honey?'
Caught in a truck's light, I was a squirrel, digging for my . . . [offers to Dorothy] MasterCard?
Caught at my job interview, with a question off guard.
She repeated again, this time slowly so I could follow,
'We don't want no illegal workers here in Straya.'
Bravo!

What makes you Australian?
Is it a Southern Cross tattoo?
Or wombat stew crumbled with a Dunkaroo?

As if my Aussie passport is temporary or my birthplace a mistake,
For all those Dorothys out there, allow me to firmly iterate:

'For those who've come across the seas
We've boundless plains to share,
With courage let us all combine
To Advance Australia Fair.'

Upon hearing these lines do you think of a time
When Australia has learnt to share and care
And dare to wear its heart on its face
Fully aware that most of us in this place
Are far from fair
But brown and black and slow to attack
But quick to embrace?
A warm Australia.
A handmade Australia.
Not a 'shooing' Australia.

When racists spit 'Osama' at my brother – I'm confused as to why?
On Australia Day when the night sky spews bigot bile – I'm left traumatised.
When a teen rips off my uncle's turban – I'm an enraged flame of pain and shame, and sorrow.
For tomorrow, when a hooning ute throws a rotten peach at my dad and screams, 'GO HOME YA BLOODY TERRORIST':
I will plead to you, Lara: where the bloody hell are we?

My people, the Sikhs,
Yeah, we have an identity
Just like you and her and him
Like Pru, and Fleur and Jim

See this hair
It's long and preened and seen
It stands for me and my choices

See that turban
It belongs here in suburban
Melbourne to Perth
And says, 'Hey mate, we're all equal on earth!'

And if it's really a competition, Dorothy,
Well, maybe I'm more 'Aussie' than you
If Aussie means equality 'cause
That turban it's noble from start to end
It's worn to defend
You and you and you and you
'You can trust me'
It says.

Sikhs in turbans came here in 1860
With camels and carts and courageous hearts
And look at the maxi taxi
We're still driving and steering this country
In offices and hospitals and even on stage
To Advance Australia Fair, page by page

So bring on the slurs and curs and scars and burrs
Take it for the team
Bring the racists into high beam
Let them spew their poison in my direction
So another won't have to cop this disaffection

Shut the gate on the hate state

When people tell me and my family to go home to where we came from,
I reply with a smile, tongue in cheek
'Mate, we've been right at home for the past 150 years
I'm not the one who's the freak, I'm fully Sikh!'

Winner of Peace

'Hi, this is Janet ringing from the Heart Foundation. Could I please speak to . . . Amaaaaar . . . amooooor . . . jiiiooot . . . Sorry, how do you pronounce it?'

'Amarjit. Sure, which one? Mr or Mrs?'

'Pardon?'

'My parents have the same name.'

All Sikh names are gender-neutral and have a distinct meaning to them. My name means 'winner of peace'. I know, big shoes to fill, right? And after thundering into my family's four-place-setting home when I was born, my loudness has continued to invade Transperth buses and trains. I've been told to keep the volume down on numerous occasions by people sitting behind me and by my friends. Not quite the 'winner of peace' I'm expected to be, although it is rather peaceful when I shut up.

Even though I was born in Perth, Punjabi was my first language. I lost that when I went to school, but my Indian accent remained. I was drawn to Steve Irwin in primary school, so I started speaking like him and now my accent is a watered-down version of a white Aussie dude.

Along with being so loud that I've actually been fined for it (while studying in Prague), I've also had this instinct from a young age to advocate for human rights – a 'fair go' for all. Whether it's on the Mandurah line where a woman wearing a hijab is being told to 'take it off', or outside the Leeming Recreation Centre where a classmate's head is being bashed against a wall, I'll be there with my megaphone and picket.

My brother, Harjit, would argue, 'Sukhjit, you're simply a rebel without a cause!'

So here I am, twenty years old and trying to find my cause, my purpose in this world, and my place in the family tree. My ancestry goes back to the war-torn mountain region that borders Pakistan and Afghanistan. My grandparents fled the city of Bannu (which is now in Pakistan) after the partition of India in 1947. My parents were born and raised in India but they left in 1984 during the third Sikh genocide. They both came from middle-class families. My grandfather was a banker and so my dad also became a banker (after quitting his engineering degree due to hazing). Dad had a science degree and Mum was one exam away from finishing her commerce degree but got whisked away in the middle of the night to be arranged-married to Dad. Papa had left India in 1978 as a bachelor to work at Lloyds Bank in Bahrain, and came back to meet Mum three days before their engagement. And just like that, they got married and left in 1984. There was immense pressure on my mother from her in-laws to change her name because it was the same as my father's. She refused, so the confusion between their names persists.

The confusion travelled with me to school, where I had an 'exotic' name of my own. My ears would perk up during roll call, when I would hear the almost ritualistic long pause between surnames beginning with 'J' and 'L'.

'Yeah, that's me.'

'Suck-gjheeet? . . . Suk-i-ji? . . . Suk-a-jit? . . . How about I call you Superjet? It's close enough.'

If nothing else, at least my Year 3 teacher made me sound like a superhero. Not all the names given to me were as glorifying. 'Suck-a-shit' was one of my least favourites. The absolute worst, though, was 'Gorilla Girl'. We all have our insecurities – mine was my hairy legs. Being a member of the Sikh faith, we can be recognised by our unshorn hair and turbans. It gives us a unique identity, and many Sikhs believe there is a practical and a spiritual purpose for every hair on our body.

Being called 'Gorilla Girl' was just one of the forms of verbal abuse I received at school. I was bullied for four years for not conforming to the high school hierarchy. Every day the number of boys terrorising me grew like an epidemic. As Head Girl of Leeming, I was deeply ashamed of the irony.

After putting on a brave face for four and half years, I decided to face all twenty-six of my bullies in a mediated environment and, I guess, performed my first spoken word piece of work. I spoke from the heart and asked for a bit of empathy.

'Most of you guys enjoy playing sport and some of you are in state teams. Imagine you are about to play in a grand final and I rock up with twenty-six of my friends and we start tormenting you from the benches. Deliberately and publicly humiliating you at what you do best. How would that make you feel? Would you be able to perform at your best? I still have the balls to act on stage and do my speeches at assemblies while you chant your little war cries, but there is a tumour inside me. No one deserves that. Not me; not anyone at this school.

'What you are doing is cowardly. Deal with your own shit. Don't use me to get the satisfaction of feeling powerful. If one girl has to stand up to twenty-six of you in front of the principal to be heard, she will. Because I have the guts to face my problems. I abide by our school motto, 'Harmony and Excellence', and I stay true to the meaning of my name. I am equal to you, whether you like it or not. I deserve to be treated better than that . . .'

I looked up from my shaky palm cards, after speaking for forty-five minutes, to find a room filled with a stunned principal, sobbing teachers, speechless friends and red-faced bullies in tears. As a result, I got an unexpected number of genuine apologies from most of the guys. The day after, the atmosphere changed in the school corridors. No longer did I feel fear or hate. The nods of acknowledgement, smiles and friendly hellos from my bullies made me realise that this opportunity to spread awareness had reaped many rewards. Finally, I was a winner of peace. The school was buzzing. I sent a clear message to my peers: *Bring. It. On.*

All Sikh boys are given the surname 'Singh' that translates to 'Lion' or 'King', and all Sikh girls are given 'Kaur' that translates to 'Prince' (not 'Princess', which many assume). After accepting my identity as a Sikh and confronting my bullies, that was the day I took my first steps as royalty. Now, every day when I leave the house, hairy as ever, I command to the world: *Judge Me. I Dare You.*

Is hairy the new sexy? Probably not, but I do everything I can to make it the new sexy. With beards evergreen and admirable, I wonder if being a hairy girl will ever be fashionable?

When I'm lying on my beach towel and the wind is blowing through each hair follicle, I feel free. People have often asked me, 'How do you deal with people staring at your legs? 'Cause let's face it, it's not the norm!' My secret is . . . sunglasses! When I've got my Ray-Bans on, I can pretend not to see the confused I-think-you've-got-fungus-growing-on-your-body-and-I'm-here-to-make-you-aware-of-it look of a passer-by. Besides, the stare only lasts for a couple of seconds until they find something else to judge. My brother once told me, 'Sukhjit, your personality should be so exuberant that no one even pays attention to your external looks because they are too in awe of your internal awesomeness.'

Now that you know I'm 'fully Sikh', you might be curious about who Sikhs actually are. Before I give you Sikhism 101, why don't we take a closer look at what it means to be Australian? Now, I'm not talking about wearing Bintang Beer singlets, eating Vegemite or being a bogan. What is the one value that the majority of Australians share? I'll give you a hint: it starts with M and originated during the World Wars.

Mateship.

Sikhs have come from a divided nation where war and conflict have shaped our identity. Australia's identity has also been defined in part through conflict, through being involved in wars overseas. Australians pride themselves on their courage and determination.

Growing up in Straya has taught me that we tend to focus on our differences rather than embrace our similarities. Can't we all try to find our common humanity regardless of diversities? After all, we all shit the same way.

If Australia values mateship so much, then where does racism fit in this noble narrative?

I read a blog of a Muslim girl living in the United States and her story really resonated with me. She decided to perform a little experiment. For one day, she didn't wear her hijab. Since it was wintertime she was still rugged up with a big scarf and beanie, which ended up covering the same amount of skin that she normally would have covered with a hijab. To her not-so-surprise, she experienced strangers acknowledging her presence for the first time ever. They smiled, nodded, sat next to her on public transport without fearful body language. She wrote: 'Apparently, the type of cloth you place or wrap around your head defines how you will be treated.'

As a teenager, I rarely wore my Punjabi clothes out in public. Even if we were going to the shops on a Sunday arvo straight after Gurdwara, I would refuse to leave the car – mortified that people would see me in my traditional get-up and think I was some sort of genie (true story, but we'll get to that later).

My eccentric mother, on the other hand, only put on Western attire for work. The rest of the time, whether door-knocking for the Heart Foundation or getting knee-high in the beaches of West Straya, she flowed proudly in her cultural dress. She's the type to see a mate in everyone. She'll creep up on you in the express lane at Woolworths – a lane you chose on purpose – point at the glass bottle in your basket and say, 'You might be having Chicken Tonight, Chicken Tonight, but I'll be making fresh curry.' Indian accent sold separately.

While doing her door-knocking rounds, she'll ask the most direct, personal and random questions, and then quickly waddle home so she can tell us a gazillion stories about all these new people she's met.

'Mum, I don't think the Heart Foundation hired you to do their detective work!'

'They're our neighbours, Sukhjit – if they don't have our back, who *will*?'

While I was busy looking 'cool', she was showing the world that you shouldn't be defined by what you wear. *Why blend in when you were born to stand out?* It's who you are on the inside that really matters.

Most Sikh men wear turbans and a minority of Sikh women have also chosen to wear a turban. It's a crown conveying an identity of royalty, grace and uniqueness. When you wear a turban, you fearlessly stand out.

Unfortunately, turbans (and hijabs) have had a negative presence in the media ever since 9/11. Muslims and Sikhs have been victims of hate crimes all over the world, especially in the West. I was still a primary school student in 2001, unaware of the racial divisions that would plant themselves in my neighbourhood and my perception of the Aussie Dream. 'G'day mate' was replaced with 'Go home, you terrorist!' and my dad's name, Amarjit, was replaced with 'Osama Bin Laden'.

When will I ever be classified as Australian?

These experiences of not belonging led my brother to research the pioneering Sikhs of Western Australia. Shiploads of camels were brought to Australia in the 1860s for transport and construction as part of the colonisation of the central and western parts of the country. Among the handlers of the camels were some Sikhs. Sikhs were mistakenly called 'Afghans', a term used for any dark-skinned turbaned person, especially if he was a cameleer or a hawker. We discovered that Sikhs have actually been in Western Australia for more than 150 years.

I don't really have a distinct physical identity as a Sikh because my hairiness seems to pass off as 'feminist' or 'lesbian' or 'just another hairy Indian'. However, I still feel the need to fight these injustices, even though they don't directly affect me. I feel attached to the first-hand racism Sikh men receive. When they experience a hate crime, I feel as though I have experienced a hate crime.

In January 2014 I decided to start wearing a turban. It ended up being an unintentional social experiment. *What was the big hoo-haa about the struggle of a Sikh male? Was it really that alienating to wear a turban?* Funnily enough, I received more prejudice from my own Sikh community than the wider Australian public. As a Sikh girl, wearing a turban challenges the beliefs of others. Everyone had an opinion and I became a hot topic in 'The Great Sikh Debate of Perth'.

'Why is she wearing that thing on her head? Great, now she's gone all religious on us.'

'So proud of her, she is finally showing us she is a religious girl. Hang on – why is she still showing off her skin?'

'Don't go around throwing your turban in my face, you fundamentalist!'

'Did you see her talking to that man? A turbaned girl must be modest at all times!'

'Her poor mother, no one will want to marry her daughter! She will die making curry for one!'

'Ew, hairy AND a turban! I like my Sikh girls skanky! Unless it's in front of my parents, then she'd better cover up!'

'Bro, she seems like the perfect girl for me now. Religious AND modern! Thank God she doesn't have any facial hair though!'

'Who does she think she is? Equality between men and women? She can take her feminist beliefs elsewhere!'

Through this experiment, I learnt we are not *just* our beliefs. A Muslim woman is not *just* her hijab. Quite like a nun is not *just* her habit or a police officer is not *just* their uniform, I am not *just* my turban. I am not *just* my hair. I am Sukhjit – evolving through my life experiences and hopefully getting closer to the actual intention of my name.

You might be wondering, how did everyday Australians react to my wearing a turban?

I was on the train on my way to university when a toddler sitting on the seat opposite pointed excitedly at me and said, 'Look, Mum, a genie! A genie! It's a GENIE!!!!!!' I chuckled. His mum went bright red and pretended I wasn't even there.

Before his mum could stop him, he ran up to me and said, greeting me with his beaming wide eyes, 'Genie, can you grant me three wishes?' As he went on to list what he wanted, I thought to myself, *We are not born racist; we are taught these differences from a young age*. My wish for the future is that people will learn to see the inner beauty in all. Then maybe we can all be winners of peace.

Turbanator

When I was in primary school, I would watch my big bro tie his turban before school. Sometimes, he would even get a late note for having a BTD: 'Bad Turban Day'. Harjit called himself: The Turbanator. Around this time, I got to go to my first turban ceremony, where we gathered as a community to commemorate Harjit's growth from boy to man.

You know what this turban means?
The folds of this fabric
Hold the head . . . of a warrior.

Papa told me:
Learn your history.
[Not her story, his story.]
Tiaar bar tiaar Sukhjit
A Sikh should always be ready.
Ready to step in like a superhero
Ready to help those in need
Ready for the fiercest fights
Hearts in mouths
Turban tied proud
We stand tall
Nirbau Nirvair
Without fear, without hate.
These layers I tie
Remind us of the qualities

That lie inside:
Courage. Strength. Unity.

You know what this turban means?
The folds of this fabric
Hold the head of a warrior.
There's *always* another layer to be tied
Another lesson to be given
There's so much more to this turban
Than its perfect precision.

These layers show us
How many things a Sikh can be:
Member of a family
A giver to community
Lover of spirituality
This is your crown, you are now royalty
As a Singh, Lion; As a Kaur, Prince
This turban is a barrier to bigotry
It says: forget the hate; you can trust me, mate.

The Grass Is Always Whiter

It's Mum's birthday and she's excited to see the latest Punjabi movie: *Mitti Wajaan Maardi*. We gather the troops, it's an excursion and a half for the Khalsa parivaar as these types of trips call for taking the trusty Tarago. It's an Aussie battler as it rattles for almost thirty minutes all the way to Hoyts Morley. The only venue for lovey-dovey Bollywood movies where we aren't the only ones with tiffin box curries, crunchy savoury snacks in trolleys and choc tops melting already.

Inside the cinema, all I hear is havoc before my eyes acclimatise and I recognise grandmas, grandpas, nieces, nephews, cousins, conversing at full volume across the auditorium: 'Kiddhaaaaaa!' ('Waaassssuppp!')

Phones buzzing and blaring the latest Punjabi tunes; ringtones vibrating startling Sikh prayers. Kids tripping over Naanis' walking sticks. Mums putting on their last-minute lipstick as if Harbhajan Mann himself is going to pop out of the screen to serenade these old aunties.

There's no shame in having a clap and cheer at random moments. Dancing is encouraged in the aisles and when those men whistle in response to an exciting Sikh-quence – even the priest joins in!

Then comes the iconic Bollywood intermission. A toilet paper roll unravels out of Mum's big brown purse to be used instead of napkins, of course. Small brown kids leave a trail of their gooey snacks in the line for the candy bar, when I hear a voice come from behind: 'Come on youse, get yourselves organised. You're holding us all up!'

'Yeah, Towelhead, get a move on.'

My big fat Punjabi party pauses for a moment. My parents don't react. I wanna morph into a tiny piece of popcorn. I feel a festering fire bubble in my belly – it burns, it stings.

I watch the rest of the movie not really taking much in. All that keeps echoing is 'Towelhead' and the salty taste of embarrassment.

We arrive home and unpack the Tarago. I take my time to ask, 'Why didn't you stand up to them?' Papa replies with a shrug, 'Why should we worry about what they think?'

Mum pipes in with her distinctive toothy grin. 'If I'm proud of my identity then no one can stop me from being me.'

Rajma

If you've ever met a Punjabi or South Asian kid, their favourite food will probably be rajma and rice. It's a hearty kidney bean curry and it is guaranteed to turn a frown upside down. I used to be able to smell my mum's rajma while walking down the road from school. I'd get close to home and get so excited because rajma was my comfort food. It was cooked after school, on a weekend or on a birthday and now it's my go-to Sunday lunch.

Serves 2–3

Ingredients

1 cup dry big pink or red kidney beans
5 cups fresh water
1 tsp salt
2 tbsp oil or ghee
1 tsp cumin seeds
1 large onion, finely chopped
2 medium tomatoes
5 garlic cloves
1 inch fresh ginger
1 green chilli or ½ tsp chilli powder
½ tsp turmeric powder
1 tsp cumin powder
1 tsp coriander powder

Method

- Soak the kidney beans for 4–5 hours
- Wash off all the water in which they were soaked (this is what causes tummy issues, so make sure you don't cook with this)
- In a pressure cooker, add your beans with fresh water and salt and close the lid
- Put it on high heat. When it reaches the boiling point, reduce the heat to low and cook for at least 30 mins
- Turn off the heat but don't open the lid just yet. Let it cool down itself and the pressure release
- Open the lid and check if the kidney beans are 80 per cent cooked
- In another saucepan, heat up the oil/ghee and add the cumin seeds then the onion
- Cook the onion on medium heat until it's brown
- In a blender/chopper add tomatoes, garlic, ginger and chilli. Blend to a fine paste
- Add the mixture to the cooked onion and keep stirring until the oil separates from the mixture
- Add turmeric powder, cumin powder and coriander powder
- If the mixture is sticking to the bottom of the pan, add a couple of tablespoons of water in the middle and keep roasting this mixture. (This mixture is called a masala and can be used as the base of nearly every curry!)
- Pour the kidney beans and water from the pressure cooker onto this masala
- Stir well and cook on low heat for 30 minutes until the gravy is smooth
- If more gravy is desired, you can add hot water from the kettle. If your gravy isn't thick enough, let the pot of rajma boil a little longer until more water evaporates
- Garnish with fresh coriander and serve with rice, yoghurt and pickled onions

Beware – this dish will make you quite farty, so it might not be a first date kind of dish.

The Khalsa Lodge

In 2004, I was ten years old – wearing hand-me-downs, being the class clown, and bringing my sick raps to Leeming town. John Howard was our prime minister, Facebook had launched into our world and I knew nothing about either of them.

I was the shyest girl at Leeming Primary and at Gurdwara, in our Sikh community. I used to hide behind my mum's scarf, sometimes even underneath her clothes. The community called me 'poonch', a tail – always attached to my mum.

I was Mum's kitchenhand. Amid the scent of sizzling onions, popping cumin seeds and bubbling black-eyed beans, I was unaware I was soaking up precious cooking lessons. My mother – her scarf infused with masala, between the stovetop and her special spice box – was Leeming's MasterChef!

Her natural habitats were the comforts of her kitchen and the veggie market. She waddled to the beat of her own dhol ('drum'). Unapologetically authentic. She spent her days giving, never taking or wanting. Always flowing proudly in her cultural dress, imprinting essential lessons upon my chest.

On the bad days, a hot bowl of veggie rice, coupled with her famous waltz, was priceless. She'd say, 'Koi na, kuch khalay. You'll feel so much better after you eat something.' Resistant to cooperate, I put on an act while secretly smiling at the rare opportunity I got to be embraced, cheek to cheek, as she danced me out of my misery. She and I were alike: the shape of our eyebrows, the shade of our lips, the mole on our right arms, the sway of our hips.

She believed, as a Sikh mother, it was her duty to feed us. To give us the energy to work hard and practise our spirituality, our Sikhi. From her, I learnt that a good Punjabi wife cooks, cleans and serves the needs of her husband. However, my lanky limbs found it hard to produce a perfect prantha without it looking like a map of Western Australia.

My parents came from a country of cohabitation where there were no locks on doors, schedules or bedtime routines. Everyone talked on speakerphone, self-care was seen as selfish, and privacy was a privilege. Day and night, the Spice Girls' melodies my older sister listened to while washing her hair clashed with the blasting prayers streaming live, pre-wi-fi, from the Harmandir Sahib, the Golden Temple, the holiest site for Sikhs. Meditating in the prayer room, Papa held his head in a bold orange turban. The neighbours knew him as Mr Singh. They'd watch him plant kangaroo paws in the front yard, balancing a loud phone call (on speaker) to Delhi in one hand and slurping a cup of homemade lemonade (with chaat masala) in the other. Or they'd catch a glimpse of him going for brisk walks down Westminster Road with his crisp business shirt, navy short shorts, long socks and New Balance sneakers. You'd never guess that a man who has worn the same tailored dark-brown pants since his Lloyds Bank days would have the same interests as white women in Freo. I'm talking crystals, yoga, meditation, superstitious beads and colour healing.

We spent a lot of time together and I miss that now. He was a stay-at-home dad for my entire childhood. I loved how the most mundane errands or activities felt like an adventure. We'd go for walks after dinner and spend them in silence. We'd go grocery shopping at the Woolies in Bull Creek or to his favourite shops like Myer or Harvey Norman on Thursday late-night shopping.

My parents' generosity often astounds me. Our home was the type that was open to all. Whether it was hosting 100-plus Sikhs for a kirtan every month or the entire Indian hockey team for a night in our cozy three-bedroom house! I recall some of them sleeping in our hallway in sleeping bags and every blanket Mum could find.

When I was in early primary school, I shared a bed with Mum. Later, I got upgraded to a bunk bed in my sister's room, but it was rare that we even slept in that bed because her room was always given to guests, and guests we had a plenty. From every international spiritual leader, preacher, academic, singer and instrumentalist in contemporary Sikh history to randoms Papa would find on the street and bring in: converts, students, refugees. I think that's why everyone in my family can strike up a conversation with anybody – because we were exposed to so many types of people with different views, values, cultures, sexualities, lifestyles and ages, from different countries and classes.

It was a small house for a big family with even bigger hearts, and if those Leeming walls could talk . . . having witnessed so many meals, debates, live performances, workshops, celebrations and community love.

After fifteen years of renting in that Leeming home, it was time to move to a new era. To build a five-bedroom house in Wellard, a suburb even further away from the city and community, with a room for each of us. No more sharing. I was finishing high school and about to begin my university days, and my appetite for privacy was far greater than ever. Less open house, fewer kirtans, no more Indian hockey team. Although we still had guests come stay, including for my brother's wedding, when the entire family from overseas gathered for that bender. And that felt full.

My peers at university didn't know where Leeming was, let alone Wellard. Someone in class asked me if I lived on a farm. Uni was the first time I saw eighteen-year-olds driving sports cars, and I learnt about Perth's 'golden triangle' of wealthy suburbs.

I eventually moved out of home and lived in different houses in Mount Lawley, Bayswater and Mount Pleasant. While my dad was in India visiting his parents, I ran away to Melbourne with $500 in my savings, an arts degree, no 'real' job, no plan and no friends. But to each house I took a bit of Leeming with me, whether it was that old Persian rug we'd had since I was a baby or that thin wooden spoon that my mum probably used to smack me with.

I came back to Wellard for a long stint during the rental crisis of 2023/2024. This time it was with a man, Perun. He experienced the Khalsa Lodge exactly like my Leeming childhood days. As if nothing had changed.

He woke up to the sounds of Papa singing kirtan. He'd drink his coffee and sit with my parents as they tuned in to the live stream from the Harmandir Sahib (this time with an NBN connection). He had to keep up with Mum's quick wit and cheeky humour as she stirred a pot of rajma. He helped Papa plant chillis in the garden, and they both sipped on chaat masala–infused lemonade. He experienced no locks on doors and probably got sick of all the phone calls on speakerphone. And he kept reminding me how similar my mum and I are. He described our relationship not as mother–daughter but as two mates who give each other shit and speak to each other like equals.

He taught me to appreciate this home, the food, and the love it gives.

50 Shades of Red

My favourite part of the summer holidays was hanging with my bestie Husveen at the annual Sikh youth camp. Husveen has the widest smile and has known me since I was a baby. (We still hang out and double date every month.) Papa would drive us to the Gurdwara in his pastel yellow '86 Toyota Corona.

We pull up to the Gurdwara, put on our white cotton scarves, walk into the white domed building, greet the white-turbaned priest, and then I sit cross-legged on the thick white sheets.

I feel a drip beneath, my tummy cramping . . . This is not like last year's camp! Not the day to be wearing crisp white board shorts from Jay Jays!! I discreetly make an exit, avoiding any potential gossip.

I'm dripping dark red droplets of pomegranate. It's official: I must be dying.

When I get home, Mum flies out of her bed, nodding and exclaiming 'Hogheya time!' My big sister, Manjit, says that this crimson river flowing between my cramping thighs is a gift from the universe and carries the responsibility of potential childbirth.

But shortly after comes the shifts, the change. Gone are the days of my lanky ways, no more cul-de-sac cricket with the kids. At Friday night dinner parties, adults tell me to close my legs. Mum makes me prep food with the boring aunties as they yap on about weddings, outfits and recipes while the men discuss politics and the economy.

I notice puffy pink pimples pollinating my face, long black hairs colonising my upper lip. Hips starting to protrude. How rude!

Manjit gives me some tips on how to wrap my hips with the magic of Punjabi outfits. Like a cocoon, this attire protects me from the discomfort of puberty. My friends always ask me, 'Is that a sari?' and I'm like, 'Nah, mate, it's a phulkari.'

This fabric woven into a flower feels familiar, like family. I feel the power of my Punjabi culture running through my fingers, with the smell of Indian threads lingering.

Inside the Gurdwara, they all look like me, dress like me, speak like me, eat like me, so I eat pray love rinse repeat, meditate, rejuvenate, safe to radiate my religion in this vicinity.

I hear harmonious hymns heal my heart. I see families giving away cartons of sugarcane sticks and mouth-watering mulberries from their gardens. Kids learning gatka, a Sikh martial art, on the grass. Grandparents greeting each other with glee. In the kitchen, volunteers rolling thousands of rotis, stirring an abundance of aromatic spicy dal. My community is my refuge from the outside world.

Until Papa insists that we must pass by Woolies on the way home. I'm reluctant to get out of the Tarago, mortified that someone from school might see me. But Mum forces me out, firmly pointing her frail finger in my face. 'Don't be shy of your colour or being different, Sukhjit. You are not like others and that is exactly how God made you: perfect.'

Preserving Mum's little pep talk, I proudly parade my inner peacock in that supermarket. I'm thrown off for a bit because instead of a checkout chick scanning tins of baked beans and Curly Wurlys, I see a golden-haired hottie from school. We lock eyes. He asks me my name. I play with my curly mane and proudly state: 'My name is Sukhjit.'

'Sorry, Sukh-a-what? I'll just call you Suki.'

Mac and Cheese

At Leeming Primary School, we got hot lunches on a Monday. I used to order the mac and cheese for two dollars, and it came with a Sunshine Punch fruit drink. I know Garfield hates Mondays but I LOVED Mondays. I used to show up to school an hour early, before my teachers had even arrived. The food would be delivered in a washing basket and the teacher had to fend us off from breathing all over it. Such keen beans! I don't think I've ever been able to re-create that mac and cheese from Leeming, but this recipe is as close as possible.

Serves 2

Ingredients
water, salt and oil to boil the pasta in
200g macaroni
2 tbsp butter
2 tbsp plain flour
approximately 1½ cups of milk (you may need more if the sauce gets too thick)
salt and pepper
shredded cheese (whatever you like – I prefer mozzarella but you can mix it with parmesan or cheddar)

Method

- Preheat the oven to 180 degrees. Cook the pasta following the packet instructions
- Put the butter in a pan on low heat and stir until it melts
- Quickly add the flour before the butter starts to sizzle and stir fast until the butter and flour join and form a clump. Break it up with a wooden spoon so it forms small balls, as they will be easier to melt into the sauce
- When the mixture starts to turn brown, quickly add some milk and quickly start beating it with a beater, making sure nothing gets burnt on the bottom. The aim is to beat fast and scrape the bottom. Mix and stir and beat really fast until you get tired of it and you don't see any more bits or balls of flour and butter. It will be so smooth you will know it's clumpless
- Remember to keep it on slow, otherwise the sauce will burn. Keep beating and soon the sauce will become creamy and smooth and not runny or watery. As soon as it starts to bubble, turn off the gas and the sauce will be done
- By then the pasta will be cooked and you can get a baking dish and mix the pasta and sauce together until all the pasta is covered with sauce. Add grated cheese on top for some taste
- Bake in the oven for approximately 15–20 minutes, but keep checking on it until the cheese starts to turn brown and sizzle

After a couple of years of me ordering the mac and cheese on Mondays, they changed the recipe by adding nutmeg. It was the worst day of my life. I hate nutmeg. If you want to ruin this recipe, you can add nutmeg . . . I guess . . .

Crush

I grew up with conflicting ideas on relationships, love and romance. At school, I idolised over the Olsen Twins and Hillary Duff and read *Total Girl* magazine with my bestie, doing all the quizzes on who my perfect man would be and studying articles on 'how to get your crush, crushing on you'. At home, however, I was watching Bollywood and Punjabi movies with my mum, where the guy would basically stalk the woman and harass her the entire movie until she gave in to him and his grand gestures of obsession through elaborate dance and song.

Even though all my friends and family know how much I loathe Bollywood and Punjabi movies, I hate to admit that these sappy storylines of stalkery unfortunately influenced my expression of romance as an adolescent.

I entered Leeming Senior High School in 2007 with my coconut-oiled bushy locks neatly plaited, white hip bands from Supre covering the crotch of my skort (for decency, of course), a tonne of SpongeBob paraphernalia, a chana masala packed in my *Little Mermaid* lunch box and a fragile self-esteem. I found 'my people' in drama class, where the weird in us was appreciated. This was also a space where cohorts mixed things up. Most of my friends throughout high school were in years above me because of our bonds during school productions.

I still remember the first day I saw Chivaun Mailata perform. He was jamming with his guitar in the music room, alone, and as I peeped in through the crack, I felt magic in my body. His soft(-looking) skin (I mean, I'd never touched it), kind eyes, and sexy tattoos on his calves . . . These were all just too much goodness for this hairy little lady from conservative Punjab. From that day onwards, I was obsessed.

I even had a nickname for him: 'my latte', because it sounded like his surname. Any school day I bumped into Chivaun was a good day for Sukhjit. I'd forget the world around me and just fantasise about him and me dancing in a field of marigolds. I would long for his gaze, his smile, a glimpse into his world. I watched him play rugby, went to all his drama and music performances. He made everything look and sound so good. Even a Jason Mraz song. He made our daggy school uniform look sexy.

In Year 9 metalwork, I made him a silver ring with his initials carefully carved out. I left it in his locker with a poem, which I recently found on my hard drive. Keep in mind, I was fourteen, angsty and had just discovered Rhymezone.com. It went a little something like this:

I know you might be thinking, who the hell is this?
but I've seen you everywhere, more than you could have missed.

I've heard you play the guitar, in the music room,
and seen you perform in a play, wearing a cute costume.

Every time I see you, walking past in the corridor,
I stare at you; my heart beats fast as I melt into the floor.

Damn, I think, I wish I actually had the guts to talk to you,
but you're way too hot for an ugly person like me, to seriously pursue.

Though this poem may sound corny and that it may seem really lame,
you might not know but you are an amazing person in every single way.

You might think what a freak this girl really is,
to write to me and pour out her freaky feelings.

I'm really sorry if this whole thing is freaking you out,
but I seriously don't know what I would do without.

Even though I've never talked to you, face to face,
I can tell that you are the sort of person, which no one can replace.

The first time I set my eyes on you, 'that really hot guy',
I wasn't going to forget that face, no matter how hard I tried.

I have been thinking of you, morning, day and night,
I can't get your breathtaking picture out of my wondering sight.

You're much too good, and not just a pretty face to me,
because you have so many talents, a lot to give, for free.

Even though I'm heaps younger than you and won't have a chance,
I think I've fallen in love with you and can't help stealing a glance.

I have no idea what you have done to me, or inspired,

but you are the one that I sincerely admire.
Love, Your Secret Admirer

(I don't know about you but I think this poem launched my career as a professional spoken word artist.) By Year 10, everyone knew I was crushing hard on Chivaun. The teachers knew. His peers, my peers, the mean girls, the drama class – everyone except him.

Like a scene from *Lizzie McGuire*, I actually watched him read the poem from afar and saw him smile. So why did I never reveal myself? Share my undying love for him? He was out of my league, as the poem goes. A common Hollywood trope. I thought I wasn't good enough or hot enough to be noticed by someone like him. So I suppressed any hope of us being a thing or of him being able to say my name correctly. I watched him graduate at the Year 12 Farewell ceremony and waved my white hanky in the wind as I said goodbye to all the moments I'd be able to check him out and have access to his beauty in my vicinity.

I still cringe at the stalker vibes I must have been giving not just to Chivaun but to every awkward crush since. I'm ashamed I was that Indian guy from my mum's movies who made grand romantic gestures to capture the heart of a hottie. The only difference is, I didn't land Chivaun Mailata and have my happily ever after. My unhealthy and borderline criminal behaviour didn't pay off. (I guess I'll just have to settle with a stolen strand of his silky hair lol jk jk)

I've always wondered if Chivaun knew my obsession for him. If so, was he creeped out? Chivaun, if you're reading this – thank you for being my first crush and teaching me how much of a romantic I am.

Now as an adult, I've found the love of my life and we've had six amazing years together. Every day we dance among the marigolds and he loves my passion and my poetry, and my expression of romance has come a long way.

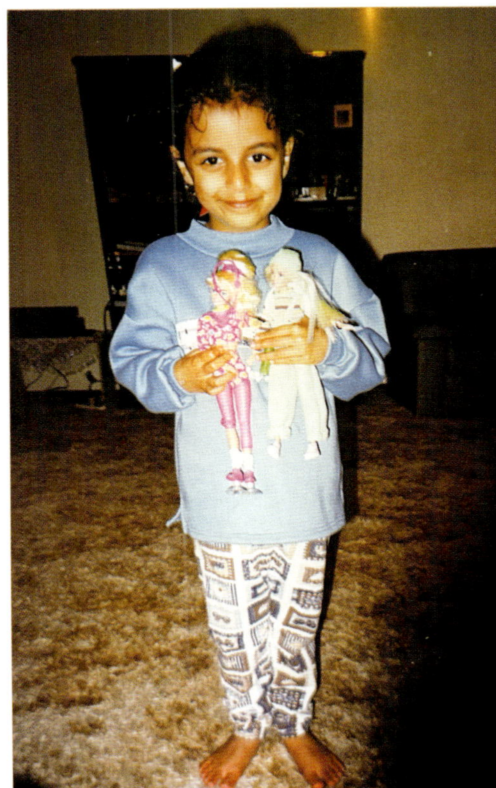

Above: Papa, me and the wide open road, 2001

Right: early field research in white feminism, 2002

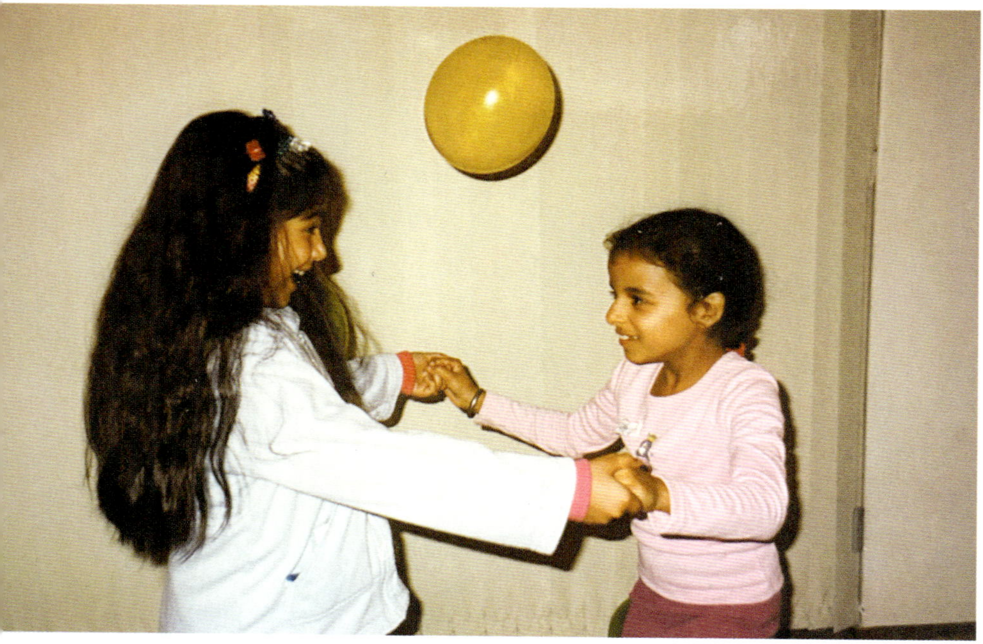

12 21 '98

Facing page: so you think you can dance, 2001

Tastes like capitalism, 1998

Right: we trusted the photographer knew what he was doing, 1999

Peeling peas in New Delhi, 2003

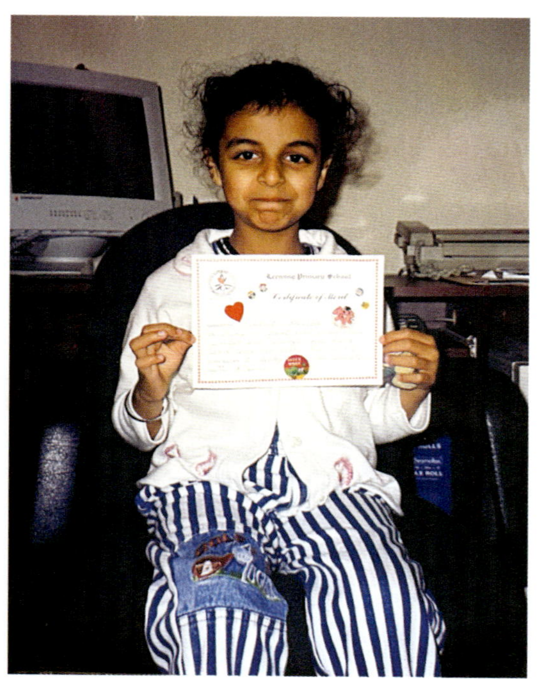

Left: got my certificate in rapping, 2000

Morning routine ft late Lou Singh Ji, 2002

Facing page: meditating with (or imitating) Papa, 2001

Chillin with my big sis, 2001

Facing page: Langar on Westminster Rd, 1999

Poor mum, 1995

Right: Princess Sophia Alexandrovna Duleep Singh (1876–1948)

Indian suffragettes on the Women's Coronation Procession, London, 17th June 1911

Above: Australia's Got Talent judges, 1994

HMS (Harjit, Manjit and Sukhjit), 1994

Facing page: in my farm girl era, 2004

My relationship with watermelon has always been intense, 2004

'04 7 19

'04 4 28

Above: a visit from the grandparents, mid-90s

Facing page: Harmandir Sahib in Amritsar, 2011

Stone carving in Bhaja Caves, 200 BCE

UWA Graduate, 2014

30th Birthday, 2024

EMERGING
WRITERS'
FESTIVAL
14–23 JUNE

EDx UWA

Facing page, top: I still own that cat dress, 2017
Tedx talk, UWA, 2016

Above: Slamalamadingdong in Naarm, 2016

Things to Consider When Bringing a Non-Sikh Partner to the Annual Family Mandurah Christmas Lights Cruise

- Is it love? Seriously, is it love?
- Test the waters, intro to Mum first. She will put in a good word with Papa
- Educate him about Sikhi, the dos and don'ts
- Show parents that he's educated (or, at least, has made an attempt)
- Have confidence in your parents that they will accept him, don't lose hope
- Get kicked out of your rental during the housing crisis and move in with your parents for a year and a half to force the love to happen

Sukhjit's Fifteenth Birthday Speech

I just wanted to say thank you to everyone for making my fifteen years on this planet special. Now I really doubt Waheguru Ji put us all under the roof of 31 Westminster Road Leeming just because he felt like it. He did it for a reason: not only to give us a test of who can make it out alive, but also because we are all meant for each other in a funky Khalsa sort of way. Can you believe exactly fifteen years ago that an amazing creature was born and enlightened your lives altogether? Because I can't!

Harjit, I've got many things from you: your witty sense of humour, your confidence, your outgoing personality and your attitude. If it weren't for you, I certainly wouldn't be the person I am today – Sukhjit the Great. We've both had our ups and downs but along this brother–sister journey I have learnt so much from you, Mister. You have done so much and made us all happy, and I know we don't say this much but we are definitely proud of you. I remember that time when Manjit and Mummy went to Melbourne and Papa was out getting some pizza. And since back in the day pizza was a novelty, we got too excited and started bouncing the AWL free extra-large beach ball around the house and suddenly it bounced too high and broke the light. I learnt two things that afternoon: you and I must really have the love for pizza, and that was the first time I ever saw you vacuum.

Manjit, as much as I don't want one, you can give me a kiss today, so it's your lucky day. One thing I must say is that you have the most influence on me and you should be in the Guinness Book of Records for being the most patient person in the world. Even though you get on my nerves twenty-three hours of the day, I still love you for that hour. Just joking – it should really be the other way around. You're a pretty amazing creature. All those projects you've stayed up all night for me to complete and all the commitments you've made for me.

Mummy and Papa, you guys are my heroes, and I'm not talking about that crazy show that Harjit watches with his bestie, Scott. I'm talking about the real deal. Without all your guidance and support I wouldn't be alive today. I love hearing your childhood stories and adventures together, which has led to moments of uncontrollable laughter in the living room.

Thanks for bearing with me for the last fifteen years. You guys have been my everything and I love you all. And all of us Khalsas have a lot of life still to get through. I can't wait to find out where destiny takes us.

Apple Cake

My parents went through a healthy phase when I was born, cutting out all the snacks, soft drinks and sugar, and they made some interesting choices when it came to baked goods. For birthdays they would make this apple cake. Dad's version was healthier than this recipe, but because I wasn't a big fan I'm going to share Mum's version, which is super classic yum!!

Serves about 8

Ingredients
120 g butter
1 cup raw sugar
1½ cup wholemeal flour
½ tsp baking powder
½ tsp baking soda
2 or 3 green apples, peeled and grated
1 egg

Topping
50 g butter
¼ cup raw sugar
½ cup rolled oats

Method

- Preheat oven to 180 degrees
- Melt 120 g butter in a pot and leave it to the side
- Sift the flour and combine with the other dry ingredients (sugar, baking powder and baking soda)
- Beat the egg and combine it with the melted butter and grated apples
- Add a drop of milk if the mixture isn't sticky enough
- Mix the dry and wet mixtures together and pour into a greased bundt tin
- Melt 50 g butter and combine with the other topping ingredients (raw sugar and rolled oats), then add to the top of the cake
- Bake for 45 minutes and serve with vanilla ice cream

ਪਰਦੇਸ Pardēs

If my childhood were a meme
it would scream: 'aajoh khaloh!!!!!!!'
with an image of Mum fearlessly
charring rotis on an open flame.
Dinner. Is. Ready.

Our culinary senses
came alive every night
when we were served an array of spicy preserves:
pickled onion, tangy tamarind chutney, cumin-y cucumber raita . . .
it was condiments galore
and meals got more and more
adventurous
as Mum got more and more
curious
of white Australia.
Aloo tikki burgers and naan bases for pizzas
graduated to mac and cheese and spicy fajitas.
However, hot chips
always had turmeric stains
thanks to Mumma McCain
who forgot to change the
pakora oil that day.

The façade of an actress and a hostess
(obsessed with Mr Bean)
Mum was a jokester
and queen of sarcasm.
She preyed on the polite.
If a friend ever stayed for a bite
she'd pretend to charge them for their dal makhani:
'That'll be $5.49, plus GST.'
And when they looked at me mortified
she'd clarify: 'Oh, that's the discounted rate for mates.'
Poker-faced, she thrived in awkward pauses
while Papa provided awkward performances
during school lunchtimes
he'd be in the front garden
kneeling and weeding
while my friends and I
paraded and masqueraded
around the school oval
like *Total Girl* goddesses.
Papa would make eye contact
I'd try and distract my mates
but I was always too late.
'Beta, tuck your shirt in!'
They saw him
all of him
as he gestured at us
topless?!?
He's still immune to irony.

On the weekend
we washed our manes
soaking up that vitamin D.
The intimacy, the ritual
of drying our thick black locks
considered pretty unorthodox
for our neighbours
as they tried to get a glimpse

through the crack in the fence.
We'd fight for the title of
'Longest Hair in Leeming'
as we hopped into the Tarago
for another weekly ritual
synonymous with
the Khalsa parivaar:
fruit picking.

Hail or scorching summer heat
we'd be at Rosie's farm in a beat.
My ears wouldn't have even popped
from the journey to the hills
and Papa would be popping
juicy loquats into my mouth:
'aajoh khaloh!'
I always wondered
where this obsession with farms and fresh fruit
came from?

Maybe it's in my roots . . .
My people, the Sikhs
came from lush landscapes
of crisp corn crops,
succulent spinach fields
and moon-lit meadows of mustard.
Where farmers were forever fortunate
for the fertile soil
that kept their families fed
in the land of five rivers.

If my childhood were a thread
it would connect all the vibrant colours
into a phulkari
and remind me
to be proud of my parivaar
my family.

Aloo Tikki Burger

Whether you're at Maccas in New Delhi or Lord of the Fries in Northbridge, you must get your hands on an aloo tikki burger. It's a great veggie option, a patty made from potatoes and sometimes other mushed-up vegetables.

Makes 8–10 small patties

Ingredients
500 g red or purple potatoes
½ cup breadcrumbs
handful of fresh coriander, chopped up
1 tsp salt
½ tsp coriander powder
½ tsp cumin powder
1 green chilli, finely chopped or ½ tsp chilli powder (or both if you love chilli)
burger buns
butter, for spreading
tomato ketchup
green chutney

Method

- Boil the potatoes then let them cool. Peel them and mash them up in a mixing bowl
- Add breadcrumbs, coriander, salt, cumin powder and chilli and mix well
- Form small patties with the mixture
- Shallow-fry the patties in a frypan on medium to high heat until both sides are brown and crispy
- Take them out and place them on a paper towel
- Assemble your burgers with desired condiments (salad leaves, baby spinach, slices tomatoes, sliced onions, grated carrot, jalapenos, etc.)

This is my favourite recipe for a weekend lunch or a Friday evening when the whole family is together. It's fun to make your own burger and sometimes I just crave eating those patties on their own with some mint chutney.

To Whom It May Concern

I was issued these bowels on 24 May 1994 at 11.12 a.m. at Woodside Hospital, Fremantle. I was led to believe that I would not suffer major defects until at least sixty years. However, I am contacting you at the ripe age of twenty-seven. Thus, I am now feeling poopy. Literally.

Let me bring you up to speed on the saga so fart . . . I mean, so far.

Unfortunately, I didn't have a say in choosing this product as it came fully installed in me when I was born. I didn't even get a chance to create a Pinterest board or do online research via Product Review. No one even gave me a user manual.

During the first seven years, the product worked as advertised. What when in, came out. I also note, potty training was as expected – messy but rewarding.

But then the malfunctions started at ten years:

- had a tub of ice cream, diarrhoea
- drunk no water for three days, constipation
- baked beans for brunch, flatulence
- ate an entire loaf of bread, bloated.

My middle name is Kauren, or Karen for short, so naturally I complained to your head office. But I was told you have a shitty returns policy. So, I took a different approach to ensure the system was well serviced. After strictly eating flaxseed, fruits and veggies, and probiotics until eighteen years of ownership, a trip to India brought on some fairly loose motions. I guess the exotic spices and foreign dairy products from the motherland didn't sit well with this Aussie engineering. I wasn't aware chana masala would be considered outside the warranty's wear and tear. As an Indian myself, I feel this heinous contradiction to be quite racist. Do bowels see colour?

I was hospitalised and immediately a hands-on investigation began. After performing a colonoscopy and an endoscopy, the surgeon said, 'We couldn't find the stick up your arse so you probably just have IBS – but you should really see someone about your attitude.' Irritable Bowel Syndrome!? It's not my fault my guts have anger issues.

Quite like the twists and turns of my bowels, Mum's spaghetti just sometimes didn't want to come out. My intestines are either exploding in rage or bottling up their fillings. They're triggered by: watermelon, mac and cheese, pasta, naan, gnocchi, muffins, pesto, onions, kombucha, juice, garlic, Coke, ice cream, gelato, ricotta, bocconcini, camembert, brie, paneer, baked beans, black-eyed peas, falafels, mushrooms, pickled vegetables, avocados, guavas, grapefruits, pomegranates, bread, breadcrumbs, cakes, biscuits, udon noodles, potato bake, lasagne, Coco Pops, couscous, roti, semolina, hummus, relishes, tzatziki, my mum's yoghurt . . . basically all my favourite things!

I have spent many hours, days, weeks in bathrooms, park toilets, fancy restrooms, shopping centre dunnies, wailing: 'How do you give me so much pleasure and cause me so much pain?'

I have found some creative sources of relief, such as coffee, which result in the sweet sweet release I long for. One may say they rectify the situation. But only temporarily.

I thought maybe group therapy could ease the haemorrhoid rips and scars. I found a couple of people in my inner circle who occasionally shit themselves in the middle of the night. Who aren't ashamed of changing their linen due to an episode. I felt less alone. We saw each other weekly, but after a month I discovered there wasn't much helpful advice my seven-month-old niece and eighteen-month-old nephew could really give me. Other than smearing their shit on the wall.

There I was, back to square one. Suffering. Not in silence, might I add. I fell in love with a beautiful man, Perun Raymond Bonser (who wishes to remain anonymous), and apparently the first time we slept in the same bed, I farted in my sleep. Now, he only told me this three months later, but you can imagine how I felt as a person who sees herself as sexy not stanky. I have been farting in my sleep every night since and it can cause quite a lot of grief in our unventilated apartment. Just the other night, Perun got a little bit of fart in his eye and it was burning for forty-eight hours. I might lose my man if you don't do something about this promptly. A lot is at stake here.

My social life has been affected by these broken bowels. Going out to eat already sucks as a vegetarian, and now that my greatest joys have been taken away from me (see list above) what am I supposed to eat? Kale? Well, guess what, I can't even eat kale. The consistency of my poos is appalling and it only gets worse when I'm on my period. Am I right, ladies?

I'd like my current bowels replaced without the shitty baggage. And please don't suggest crappy solutions like exercise, the FODMAP diet and meditation as they clearly won't work. If you do not heed my request, I will have no other choice but to unionise and start my own bowel movement.

Regards,

Sukhjit

Mein Hair

My first week in Melbourne
On a train far from Malvern
My ears perk up as I hear a man tell his mate,
'Woahhhhhh hairy legs! Did you see that, Dave?'

From age nine
I was taught to hide
My hair
As if my body were a questionnaire.
Papa glanced at my legs and told me
It was best I start wearing pants now
As I was too old now
For flippy skirts from Supré.
For board shorts from Jay Jays.
Brought up in a secluded world
Unaware of Western shaving habits
I grew up believing
White girls weren't born with leg hair.

Not conscious of my hairiness
Until a boy in Year 8 narrated:
'Hey everyone, look, its Gorilla Girl!
Looks like a jungle growing down there!
You have the hairiest legs in the world, man.'
Guinness World Records HAIR I come!

Why aren't I like everybody else?
Why don't I feel feminine?

My questions were triggered by ads
In which models would caress their photoshopped legs
Exclaim in voices sweeter than a lotus emerging from my uterus,
'Veet: what beauty feels like'.

Am I not a beautiful girl?

So the time came.
Shaver in one hand, a dollop of cream in the other.
I nervously shaved fourteen-years' worth of leg hair
Watching my religious beliefs slowly go down the drain.

The bullies? Won't stop
They can't stop [sung in Miley Cyrus way]
And I had to put a stop on this double life.
Hiding my smooth legs from my family
Or hiding my hairy legs from the world
I chose freedom.

'Hey buddy, were you talking about my hairy legs?'
He replies to me but appears to be muttering to his friend.
He had been in jail for five years for armed robberies.
He had been divorced three times.
But never had he seen a 'chick' with hairy legs
'I thought you were a dude and then I looked up and I saw a beautiful woman.
Girls don't have hair. They shouldn't have hair. You'd look so much better without it, just saying.'

I had some business to take care of
Some people to make aware of
Some men to educate.
As a lesson in femininity and
Redefining beauty
Was about to take place.

See, for a long time, I saw my hair as a curse.

Sometimes it was bushy, rough and big
Some days it was soft, silky and straightened
But it's always been black and very, very, VERY long.

When I was a little sapling in school
They would pull and I clutched
They laid eggs and I itched
They would massage oil and my scalp would smell for weeks
Every morning, Mum would run after me in our suburban backyard
I would squeal with resistance like a piglet about to be captured for slaughter.
She pulled and pulled my strands like a rope on a sail
'Shhhh, stop shrieking, our Aussie neighbours will think I'm abusing you or something!'

The expired coconut oil slid through my curls, deranging them into grease clots
Even my friends would avoid sitting next to the bubble of,
'What's that gross smell? Like, ew.'
Ask my hair.

When I sprouted throughout puberty
They would plait and I would set free
The shrubbery
Of my teens
So when I reached university
Where people embraced diversity
I could ask the boys: 'Do you want to get lost in these wild curls of mine?'

When people catch a glimpse of my hairy armpits, they assume I'm lesbian or a feminist.
I guess I'm definitely one of the two.
After all, it takes a Miley Cyrus to take armpit hair off the list of taboo.

However, getting bullied was the best thing that ever happened to me.
It prepared me
For moments like these on a Melbourne train.

The people looked up from their gadgets
This was better than an episode of *My Kitchen Rules*
Because the rules of my upbringing were to speak up
To be a lion not a lamb.

We talked of embracing differences and freedom of expression
How the ink on his arms was his way
And the roots weaved on my body were mine.
Sikh and You Shall Find

You have to understand the way I am,
Mein Herr.
A tiger is a tiger, not a lamb,
Mein Herr.
But my mane
Will remain
Mein
Hair.

Roar Like a Kaur

To all my allies,
When you say you respect women
Do you mean ALL women or just
'Your woman'?

If you want to enjoy the array of this babin' buffet
Know that it's not about treating your mumma with respect
And forgetting about the rest of us
Constantly rejecting this conversation
I'm getting tired with your defensiveness.

It's time to listen, my brothers.
Take a seat.
It's time to unlearn my fathers.
And practise what our Gurus preached.
It's time to make some room for women in this world.
Because this toxic masculinity and dominance has been taking up too much space.

Your WhatsApp jokes about Coke-bottle figures,
Mr Yo Yo Honey Singh,
Don't be surprised when I snigger
At 'Lak 28 kudi da, 47 weight kudi da'

For how long will you objectify this body?
That was given to me for productivity
Not just reproductively.
For how long will you shame?
And victim blame
And name call
And rape
And abuse
And shun our voices
Constrict our throats
No master
I'm not your genie in a bottle
So if you rub me the wrong way
You better
Have an apology ready
If you want to stay.

You can call me princess
You can call me queen
And serenade
And protect and provide
But know that I won't be happy until I'm seen as an equal.

People sigh and say, 'Well, what can we do?
Men won't change, you just have to accept it, it's not an area to pursue.'
The day we start accepting these battles as the norm, is the day we give in.
Throw in our chequered tea towels and floral aprons to a community I believe has sinned.

Let female existence be blamed for lust in a man's mind,
Instead of encouraging self-control in his daily grind.
I don't believe you and I are any different, we were created to coexist.
Yet these double standards continue to persist.
My freedom to express
Is quickly oppressed.
Does wearing a dress

Make me less
Of a Sikh?
Where's the inner spirituality
If I can't progress
Because society is obsessed
With the outer?
I guess I'm a temptress
As I caress
My long hairy legs, arms, neck and shoulders,
It becomes seductive anatomy, nonetheless.

Well, guess what?
Our wombs have been traumatised from killing all the daughters

I urge you to sit with your sons and show them a tampon
A pad
A menstrual cup
And explain
We aren't dirty
We aren't impure
We are preparing our bodies
To endure and produce your children

If a Sikh is constantly learning, why not learn how to speak up for your allies
Because you know how it feels to be marginalised.
To be judged based on your external
So next time you are confronted by my appearance
My attitude
My dress
My hair
My being
My mind
Know that I will continue to fight for your rights
Despite your hateful messages and ignorance
I will always protect you, with diligence.

For some, freedom comes with owning a vehicle
For others, it's driving that vehicle
For me, it's being the vehicle

And this vehicle can taste freedom.
No fear because freedom is here.

Crikey

I found an Aussie slang dictionary in Ishka (a weird Indian fetish store in Melbourne) and wrote a poem using every single word in the book.

One morning
After the Chrissie hols
I wake up a bit iffy.
At this time
The weather down under
Is dry as a dead dingo's donger.
Kookaburras are crying
And I'd been grindin'
My choppers during my slumber.
Unlike my old man
Who's up at sparrow's fart o'clock
Has a cheerful cuppa with some toast and avo on top
Says 'G'day' to the chippie next door
Who replies with a 'nippy morning aye!'
'Matty, are you talking clap trap?'
As he wipes his sweat with a snot rag
They share a beer belly laugh and chinwag
About Don Bradman and Ian Thorpe
The true-blue Aussies they are
Everything's hunky-dory with this story
Until we head indoors.

I'm in my bed playing possum
While I can hear them waffle on.
Still in my jammies,
I crawl to the mirror. I quiver.
My face looks like a festered pickle
I'm basically chopped liver.
I've been on a bad trot
With this puberty thingo.
I don't feel too crash hot,
Must have been last night's chew and spew.
'Cause I had the dry rots this morning
Hope I can pull through.

In due time my sis, the airy-fairy type, screams from the loo,
'Pong, Sukhjit, I can see a floater in the lavvy!'
She's pretty savvy with my dodgy moves.
She mutters, 'I can't wait to leave this coop
So I never have to deal with all of you fruit loops.'

In other news
My bro and I get into a blue
Over the shower use. I win! What a ripper!
Ta bro, I'll try my best to make it snappy.
Meanwhile, Mum's multitasking in the kitchen.
Yapping on the dog and bone with her rellos
Teeing up tea parties
And firing away fashion advice.
She hasn't yarned with the bush telegraph in yonks.
Papa honks his yellow '86 Toyota Corona.
'Hang on a tick, Amarjit.
You're acting like a jack in the box
I'm flat out like a lizard drinking
Been making nibbles since five o'clock.
If you don't wanna blow your dough on festival food
And be a tight-arse and get in a hangry mood
I suggest you settle, petal
And help me look for the bottle of dead horse.

I've got mushies for the jaffles
Lamingtons for the kiddywinks
Is there anything else missing?'

'She'll be right, love
We can always pop into the servo.
Now rattle your dags
Get the kids in the car
We're gonna be late!'

It takes a jiffy and a half
But then we're off like a bucket of prawns in the hot sun.
Being cramped in Dad's Corona isn't that fun
I'm always in the middle seat.
It starts with a niggling nudge then a big shove
Turns into a tiff over nothing.
'Shut your bunghole, Sukhjit, you're dropping big clangers
The Harbour bridge isn't called a coat hanger.'
No need to get all berko, bro,
I heard it on the idiot box – the tellie
I'm just having a friendly dig, ya wally.
'Stop yanking his chain'
I can feel Mum's ears flapping
'Don't spit the dummy, you two.
No need to carry on like a pair of pork chops
If you don't stop, I'll fart a crowbar.
I present to you my kids – the flamin' galahs!'

Harjit chucks a sook
Strewth, so sensitive.
Can't even hack a serve of verbal diarrhoea
From his blood relative.
Before I spill my guts
Mum cuts me off, 'Don't you dare give me lip, missy!'
I look to my sis for support
Who's resorted to headphones

Ignoring our episode
Blissfully bopping to the bridges of the Backstreet Boys.
The brake squeaks as we pull up at the traffic light
A bunch of bad-news brothers
Howling, 'Aussie Aussie Aussie – oi oi oi!'
From their green ute.
Pops gives his cricket lingo a bash:

'She's a beaut ute. How's it going, mate?'
They stare at us like pick pocketers at a nudist camp
There's something funky in their eyes
That doesn't look quite right
So I tell Dad to fang it.
But these aggro blokes aren't done with the convo.
The ratbags start chucking lemons.

'I'm too long in the tooth to get in a scruff'
The bludger's putting dings in our car
Old man's spewing,
'I don't' wanna get in a bingle
So let's chuck a U-ie
And escape these face aches.
I think I've made a mistake
For saying "G'day".'

Before we get a chance to nick off
One of the hoons growls,
'Go home, you bloody terrorist'
Another shouts,
'I'll knock that towel off ya head
With a bunch of fives
If you're not careful.'
We pull over outside a Bottle-o.
The oldies' faces are fearful
I try not to cack myself
From this sudden attack.

My bro gets out in a huff
He's a goner.
Like a cut snake, he grunts,
'We put in the elbow grease
To be the bee's knees of this country.
Don't we deserve a fair go?
Where's our fair shake of the sauce bottle?'

'It's ok, son. They're just having bit of fun.
Innocent gasbagging – it's rare as hen's teeth
In this ace country.
Just tell me, Harjit,
What's the damage on my baby?'
While the men carry on about the Corona
My eyes notice a local rag on the ground
That states today is 'Australia Day'.

Mum pipes in,
'Our adventure has had a bit of a kick in the teeth
'Cause of those bloody hoons.
If we wanna make it to the fireworks
We're gonna have to hoof it
Even though my pegs are crook!'
Onya, Mum. Let's soldier on!
Suss out 'Australia Day'
To see what all the fuss is about.

Our fam finally rocks up late arvo.
Great galloping goannas,
The foreshore's packed to the rafters!
Chockers with every Tom, Dick and Harry with their Eskys
There's bit of a kerfuffle going on
More arse than class
I see larrikins taking leaks in the bush
Blokes in trackie dacks sculling amber fluid.
Sheila's in their togs, thongs and war paint
Happy little vegemites playing aerial ping-pong and cricket. Howzat!!

Couples making sheep eyes at each other.
Oldies with five o'clock shadows munching on chockie bickies
Yabbering on about their recent Bali belly.
Bogans' barbies burning their bangers
Looking like a dog's breakfast. Fair dinkum.

But like a pimple on a pumpkin – we stand out.
The crowd gawks at us
But Mum and Dad don't give a whoop.
I feel a bit funny in my breadbasket.
Green around the gills, hope I don't hurl.
I race to the nearest thunderbox
While my fam look around for a good possie.
Colonising a patch of grass,
They set up camp slap bang in the middle of the action.
Manjit goes for a gander to avoid embarrassment.
Harjit doesn't look like he's having a wallop of fun either.
The 'rents are knocking their socks off-
Tucking into their tasty tucker.
But I don't have an appetite.
I'm buggered! Knackered.
Got mozzies biting me all over.
I wanna get outta here, hit the hay
So I hide in the dunny
Catch forty winks
And try to forget about this bomb of a day.

ਪੁਸ਼ ਦਿਲ *Kush Dil* / Happy Heart

I arrive at JFK
after twenty-nine
endlessly elongated
uneventful
hours.

I walk through Manhattan
re-enacting all those childhood movie scenes
I climb the buildings and bridges
taking in this iconic city
I taste every bagel, pretzel,
pizza slice and local delights
but what I'm surprised to find
is your Queens home
is where my heart feels happy.

I see a tapestry of cultures
vibrant, bold
characters in conflict
unfolding their stories.
I feel the comfort of chaos.
My inner monologue
quickly switches to an old white guy
venturing through exotic lands
narrating his journey

to find the best masala chai
or something spicy like that.
The Guyanese cuisine sets the scene
as Punjabi pughs pulsate in Nissan Pulsars
Reggae melodies morph into the night
all intertwined
like a symphony of tongues.
I'm envious
of this country
where each sub-culture
has space to find its home.
I'm relieved to escape
the pasty panorama of Perth
upholding uptight British politeness
so I embrace the freeing (yet polluted) air
slowing expressing
my true desi self.

We blast Babbu's *Red Gaddi Challenger*
on the way to the kids' swim class
whizzing past store names and street signs
that blow my mind
Gurdwara Avenue
Lassi Corner
Apna Bazaar
Singh Farm
Satgur Signs
King and Queens Punjabi Jutti
Where the bloody hell am I?

We walk the malls of Flushing.
The American Dream
screams at me from all angles
Marshalls and Burlington sweating consumerism by the kilo.

My trip coincides with a nagar kirtan
a swarm of Punjabis buzzing

I hear blaring kirtan and katha
stalls of jalebi, kulfi, pani puri
we push through thousands
waiting in laborious lines
for mouth-watering chole bhature
while boys and men stare at me
with that Delhi death stare.

I feel my mum's big chef energy
channelling through my body
as I spend most of my days in the Big Apple
cooking scones, pesto and dal makhani
chopping fresh watermelon and mint
sharing my love language with my kin.
I forage for Aussie favourites from Queens library
to read to your children
I try on your salwar kameezes and anarkalis
feeling more and more beautiful
with each glittering chunni.
I cook my famous veggie lasagne for your extended family
we sit around your firepit sharing poetry
and childhood tales
sipping on ginger ale and flavoured bubbly water
swaying on your porch swing like separated sisters
you get teary-eyed as your firstborn reads from the heart
I feel special for witnessing priceless family memories.

While your toilets might swirl the other way
and my time with you has only been seven short days
I want to subscribe to your Queens way of life
my mannerisms were once deprived
but now my mother tongue has come alive.
I long for this feeling of both ease and excitement
so I'll carry your love and these memories with me
next time I sit with my own Aussie family.

Vegetarian Lasagne

There is one thing I am known for in my family and it's my famous vegetarian lasagne. I learnt this recipe from my mum when she was working at a café in Fremantle. Fun fact: John Butler and his family have eaten this lasagne at Mum's cafe!!

Serves 3–4

Ingredients
Red Sauce
1 large onion, diced
dash of olive oil
fresh crushed garlic, to taste
fresh chillies, to taste (obviously some like it hot e.g. me)
1 tin diced Roma tomatoes
all your favourite veggies: baby eggplant, zucchini, all the colours of capsicums (red is my fav), mushrooms, baby spinach, carrot, corn, etc.
dried Italian herbs
salt and pepper, to taste
1 tsp sugar (optional)

White Sauce
4 tbsp of butter, salted or unsalted
4 tbsp plain flour
approximately 3 cups milk, depending on how thick or thin you want your white sauce
fresh basil
grated cheese (mix of mozzarella and cheddar)

1½ packets lasagne sheets

Method

Red Sauce

- In a large pot heat the olive oil, add onion and stir till transparent and verging on brownness
- Add the garlic and when it starts to become aromatic add the fresh chillies
- Chuck in the tin of tomatoes and cover the pot
- Chop up all your veggies into cubes and add them to your red sauce
- Add the herbs, salt and pepper, and if you want to take the tang out also add a teaspoon of sugar
- Put the red sauce on low heat and stir occasionally to prevent sauce from sticking to your pot
- Preheat oven to 180 degrees

White Sauce

Now, the white sauce is pretty hard for me to write down quantities for as this was the first thing my mum taught me how to make, so quite like in Indian cooking I've been taught to guestimate.

- Put a spoonful of salted or unsalted butter (doesn't really matter) on low heat. Wait till it's melted but not burnt and add the plain flour
- Add enough plain flour to give the mixture a bread crumb texture, drizzling the flour with one hand and stirring the mixture with the other

- Once the mixture is crumbly and starting to get toasty (but not too dry – it's alright if it's more buttery, though) add a cup of milk
- Turn the heat up and start whisking till your body shakes/the butter–flour mixture dissolves into the milk
- Depending on the quantity you're making, it may take a while for the mixture to become smooth and creamy. If it starts boiling and is wayyy too thick, keep adding more milk. Some like it thick and some like it thin
- Remember to never leave this sauce alone. Keep whisking or stirring because it burns easily and once it's burnt you can't really save it
- Once you've brought the sauce to boil, turn off the heat. By now your red sauce would have started to bubble as well
- Try both sauces and check for salt
- Add fresh basil to the red sauce once it's done

Layers

- First, spread a layer of white sauce into your casserole dish, so it'll be easy for your lasagne to be taken out
- Then place a layer of lasagne sheets in the dish (if they don't fit your dish then crack them into larger pieces)
- Put in a good amount of your red sauce and veggies to cover the sheets
- Pour a drizzle of white sauce then add a drizzle of cheese
- Repeat the previous steps until the dish is almost filled to the top
- At the end, add a layer of lasagne sheets and the remaining white sauce exactly like you did on the bottom, completely covering the entire dish with no sneaky bits showing
- Put heaps of cheese on top – don't hold back!
- Bake for 30 mins and then check on it to see if it needs longer. Mine usually takes 30–45 mins
- When you turn off the oven, leave the lasagne in for it to set
- Wait some time before cutting it as it might be a bit sloppy
- Serve with fresh basil on top

Two Hands

Hands up if you watch the news every night
And can't decide between fight and flight
Or might is right
Hands up everybody
And wave 'em in the air
Like you just . . . care.

He told me, my bro
Leave this earth better than at your birth
When you go
So I look at these hands
Two brown hands.

One day
I heard my mum say
My name
Sukhjit
It means winner of peace
So I thought I had to be a
Political feature
A spiritual preacher
Anything but this . . . hairy-legged creature
Then I saw the hands.

My big sister said,
'Hold my hand behn baby
And look with me
When you gaze at this country, what do you see?
Do you see stats or spirits?
Do you see boundless plains or borders?
Do you see the stars
As Southern Crosses or Seven Sisters?'

My hands have hope
So don't protect me from the world, Papa
My hands, like yours, are for working, Papa
Come build with me
An empire of empathy

Friends, hold my hand and walk the streets with me
Do you see the superheroes?
Everyday white, black and grey?
Curly and straight
Giving the time of day
Helping me on my way
Laughing and
Having their say
Teaching their kids
Like I'll teach mine
To tend and mend and spend
The time
On another
A stranger is not always danger
So wave those hands
Wave hello
Shake those hands.
Shake 'em off yo
Use those hands to touch not type or 'like'
Or emoji wink 'you're alright'
You'll feel the love and compassion
That no text can provide

Take a stand, hands
They're yours
I might be the wordsmith
But with your applause
Action this poetry
And find your cause
Join this kuri from Perth
On a mission to leave this earth
Better than she found it
At her birth.

Turban Fan

This is a rap I wrote with a young Sikh guy in Melbourne after seeing him on the news in 2016. He was bullied on the bus for wearing a turban. We performed this rap and made a music video.

See this thing
This thing I wear?
It's a turban, mate
It covers my hair

You can have a look
Maybe you'll stare
But listen to his story
And you might just care

I started to wear it
When I was a kid
Age one Mum tied
On she did

Bit later I thought
What's this all about
No other kids wear 'em
I began to doubt

So Mum sat me down
Said listen, son
Gonna tell you a story
'Bout the number one

We got one Earth
One moon, one sun
We got one heart
And we speak with one tongue

And there's one more one
And that makes the sum
There's one life force
In everyone

Each ant cat dog
Tree grass bird germ
Each girl kid man
Mum snake and worm

Each white brown yellow black
Curly or straight
Every tall short fat
Slow early or late

We are all one
I'm telling you, son
We are all one
So said my mum

Now in this world
You're gonna meet two sorts
Equal thinkers and they're pretty good sports
But hating dudes, they got fearful thoughts

You'll meet them each
And everyday
And those haters gonna hate
To quote Tay Tay

So when the haters hate
Don't cringe and cry
Don't cross your heart
And don't hope to die

Just hold your ground
With two feet firm
No need to shake
No need to squirm

Remember one thing
From now til you're dead
Why you wear
That thing on your head

It's nice for your hair
That's neat that's fine
But really that turban
Is a neon sign

The sign says
Look now – loud and proud
Look at me pick me
I'm seen in the crowd

It's a satellite dish
A glare attractor
The best antenna
As a matter of factor

I'm the one you notice
I don't run I can't hide
If you need to spew your hate
I'll take it with pride

Get it out of your system
Take it out on me
So all the other kids
Can get off free

I'll take your worst
It don't matter to me
'Cause I got a turban and
It makes me free

We have grown-ups
But they tend to shirk
So it's up to us kids
To make this country work

We can't really blame 'em
They're working and owing
No time to consider
Where this country is going
But you do, son
Said my mum
'Cause on your head
You wear a turban

So I remember the fellas
Who went before
Who stood up, not down
Then stood some more

So I said, Mum
I reckon it's fair
I'm good with this thing
On my hair

I'll be tough, I'll dare
And people can stare
To help build a country
For all to share

It's hard for those kids
Who don't have a choice
Who don't have a mum
And don't have a voice

I gotta be it for them
And more
So the cops and the media
Won't ignore

I'm a lightning rod
I live in the storm
I'm a lightning rod
In turban form
I'm a lightning rod
For hate and mean
I recycle that badness
To keep this place clean
So if you see me
And you care
Think one, think different
Just think aware

Smile or nod
Woman or man
So we know who is
A turban fan

Dear Mr Abbott

Parody of 'Cosby Sweater' by Hilltop Hoods
Co-written with Amy Vowles
Written at the height of Tony Abbott's tumultuous prime ministership

I'm a simple white girl in a nice suburban house
Got an iPhone, Wi-Fi, heterosexual spouse,
Got a uni education BUT
My commiserations
To those unhappy
Being girt by sea.

Surfing the wave
Of inequality
Thanks a lot, liberals
'n' Uncle Tony
There ain't no party
Like a capitalist orgy!
Sitting in ya throne
Ya Jurassic phoney

Lend me your ears, you got enough to go round,
So share this once, if you ain't too proud,
I know what you are – you spoilt brat
Got it all without toil – you privileged twat
If you've got a toy, they can't have it too?
So gays getting married is like World War 2?
'Cept you can't drop a nuke, cause it's 2014
Instead ya just sit there and be mean!
Their love isn't real, their love isn't true,

Unlike what you have with Murdoch newspaper group.
And don't get me started on the ABC
What world would this be without public tv?
And I don't like it
And I don't like it
And I don't like it
And I don't like it

(Ik, do, thin, chaar)
[one, two, three, four]

I feel that Tony Abbott
Should rethink his shit habits
Straya's government strayin' from what's important
The rich are getting richer, the poor are in the ditches
Discrimination, Tony's makin' all of us his bitches

Wearing them budgie smugglers
Wearing them budgie smugglers
Wearing them budgie smugglers
Wearing them budgie smugglers

Squandering resources, it's nauseous to see
Rich pockets getting fatter, while they cut down trees.
Are you daft, Tony, or just refusing to see
The absurdity of lacking sustainability
Do you not understand today's reality?
Does your McMansion survive in deep sea?
Save the Reef with Control + C?
Listen to Greenpeace, can't eat currency.
Mr Abbott don't care 'bout humanity
You don't blaze at 420, you screwin' the G20.
Like Hermione ya gotta sort out your priorities
Instead of sucking cock of the rich white minorities.
Now put a cork in your ass and stop that policy flow
Starting caring about your peeps, stop chasing that dough
I'll say this for Tony, he's got a huge dick

Cause you can't fuck a nation
With a pint-sized prick

And I don't like it
And I don't like it
And I don't like it
And I don't like it

(Ik, do, thin, chaar)

I feel that Tony Abbott
Should rethink his shit habits
Straya's government strayin' from what's important
The rich are getting richer, the poor are in the ditches
Discrimination, Tony's makin' all of us his bitches

Wearing them budgie smugglers
Wearing them budgie smugglers
Wearing them budgie smugglers
Wearing them budgie smugglers

A burqa's offensive but your ballsack isn't
Cause smuggling budgies is your life's MISSION.
I want democracy, I got
Tyrannical majorities.
I want an equal world
I get mar-gin-a-lised societies.
I want a damn fair go
I get boat people? JUST GO.
I don't care who you think you are, I care what you do,
I care that you're sending little kids to Nauru.
Perpetrating fear 'cause the other should be hated
You backward thinking, mate, it's outdated.
Wake up, bro, smell the kangaroo paws,
Instead of holding us in your nasty claws

Cause poor people are evil, aren't they, Joe?
Hockey, ya shocky, ya classist prick:
What treasurer can't measure a fair budget.
Lucky bogans can't drive 'cause if we could
Guess whose fat arse would be under the hood?
You circle-jerk to coal but can't stomach the dole
Poor people should stay in their nasty lil holes
Jules called you Mr Rabbit, which is pretty spot on,
All the fucking you do should mean you breed like one.

Elitism is cool, elitism is great,
Let's all be elitists! Why not segregate?
Yeah nah, mate, how 'bout democracy?
A voice for all and education for free,
So yeah, you're a hit with old men wearing ties,
But in generation Y that shit don't fly,
(Your policies are for people that are soon gonna die)
Racism, elitism and misogyny,
Ain't got no place in the future of society,
So run your mouth for now 'cause when you up and leave
We're taking back (control) of our motherfucking country.

Monga Khan and the Humble Hansons

The hawkers of Toowoomba followed the aroma
Of the billy can bubbling to boil
Brewing buckets of black tea for the attendees
As this meeting was about to proceed.

Dev Singh gnawing on his dry damper
Crumbs falling into his tousled beard
Closed his eyes and wailed,
'I miss my wife's makki roti and saag
I miss her singing in raag
As I peddle my horse and cart
Punjab's where I left my heart.'

The men snorted to laughter resorted
The sugarcane cutter, Karam
Hushed the crew,
'He's new to this land, give him time and a hand.
Remember what it was like for you too?'

Ghanda Singh belched, as if to agree
'I'm sick of the snarl of the Brits
Beaten to the bone
This policy of the white man is horrendous
The gorey politicians want us to go home!'

They roar of injustice galore
The back of hand
The sideways stare and full-on glare
The browny blacky mocking cocking
The difference between us and them.

'I've got a name – it's Singh,' they said
'I'm a lion, ma'am, not a boy'
Then another name got dropped
'Monga Khan'
Could raise their faces to joy

What would he do?
In the face of adversity
How did he become the legend
From the bush up to the city?

The fellows started singing the songs of Monga
That hawker and hard worker
More handsome, gentler, kinder man
A helper never a shirker.

'Wasn't he the one who delivered a camel's baby?'
'I heard he wrestled a black-headed python'
But the time he saved that Hanson child from drowning
That's a story worth reminding.

The boys leaned in and cupped an ear
Sipping their tea but silent
Wanting needing again to hear
Of Monga, brave and defiant.

The Hansons were a humble family
So the stories told
Had come out here on a boat, of course
When their littlest was not so old.

If they saw something crook or cruel
Mr Hanson said, 'Please explain?'
'My heritage was a mixed,' he said
But that didn't matter, 'cause now they were Strayan.

When headlines shouted 'Yellow Peril'
The little Hansons would stand to attest
'Wasn't Aunt Peggy an Eastern feral?
Which is why we loved her the best!'

They crossed paths with the Great Monga
On a toasty day in March
Mrs was frying Hanson's favourite
A batch of fish and chips, packed with starch

As she stooped to serve the fillet of batter
She noticed their little one gone
'Our Bonnie!' she cried, 'cause it was a screaming matter
'She's gone she's gone she's gone!'

To the river they ran
All the water arising like hearts a-pounding with muscle
Never did they imagine losing their daughter
To the rapids of River Russell.

Not a soul to witness Bonnie gasping for breath
A little way down the line
Until Monga entered to do a dance with death
Caught her dress in the nick of time.

He'd learnt how to swim in rivers much faster
Himalayan and icy and wide
When those streams hit the plains of his Indian range
His father threw him in from the side.

Now his brown hairy hand held that little pink dress
Not a thought for himself in behaviour
As he dragged her to the bank, as his father he thanked
Bonnie looked at her black-bearded saviour.

The family now cuddled, all oohed and befuddled
When he delivered young Bonnie back to them
'Not a word can we say
To thank you today, Khan sir, Monga sir
What's your way?'

'Say the way to repay'
The Hanson man begged him
'For a lifetime to you we're indebted'
'It's nothing,' said Khan, with a wave of his arm
'Just remember we're always connected'

So Monga rode on with his cart and horse
That chapter was finished, of course
Till the next act heroic from that Punjabi stoic
Leaving nothing behind for remorse.

The meeting fell silent as their favourite tale ended
And they sipped on their chai once again
'So at least there is one,
Among the white throng
Who love us,' said Dev, with a grin.

'As long as they recall that rescue from the pool'
Ghanda said, with a snort
And Karam piped in, moved his hand from his chin
'Spread the word, Hansons – we're not such bad sorts!'

Makki Roti and Saag

Sikhs come from Punjab in Northern India, where most families have farming backgrounds. My family ancestry doesn't have farming it in (maybe that's why I can't keep plants alive or grow coriander!) but the food we eat still originates from that lifestyle and diet. This recipe of flat cornbread and slow-cooked hearty greens is a great winter dish that gives you the energy to plough those fields (or, in my case, have a long nap).

Serves 2–3

Ingredients

Saag

1 large bunch English spinach
1 bunch mustard leaves (but kale is a good alternative in Australia)
½ cup water
½ inch ginger, grated
5 garlic cloves
1 green chilli
1 tsp salt
1 tbsp besan (chickpea flour)
2 tbsp ghee
1 small onion, finely chopped

Makki Roti
1 cup fine polenta
¼ tsp salt
a pinch of ajwain seeds
1 cup boiling hot water
oil or ghee to pan-fry
served with butter on top

Method

Saag

- Wash and roughly chop the spinach leaves
- In a heavy-based saucepan, add half a cup of water and the spinach and mustard leaves
- Add ginger, garlic, chilli and salt and cook it on medium heat for at least 30 minutes with the lid on
- Occasionally stir and see if there is enough water
- Make a paste with the besan (chickpea flour) and 1 tablespoon of water, then add it to the greens mixture
- With a handheld blender, blend the entire mixture until smooth
- On low heat, cook the mixture until the flour taste is gone. This should take 15–20 minutes
- In another pan, add ghee and heat up
- Add finely chopped onion
- Cook until onions are transparent
- Pour the onion–ghee mixture into the large pot of saag
- Add more chilli and butter/ghee for taste

Makki Roti

- In a bowl, mix together the polenta, salt and ajwain seeds
- Make a well in the middle of the dry mixture and pour half a cup of hot water from the kettle
- With a fork, mix everything together and if required slowly add the remaining hot water to turn the mixture into a soft dough
- Let it sit for 15–20 minutes. It will be ready to mould when it's cool to touch
- Gently knead the mixture in the palm of your hand or with a flat spoon

- When it forms a sticky dough, get a clean plastic bag or cling wrap. Pour a few drops of oil onto the cling wrap then take a golf ball–sized piece of the dough and pat it down until it forms a flat bread. The thickness of the bread should be around 2–3 mm.
- Heat up a non-stick or tawa pan, then lift the cling wrap with the bread and gently flip it onto the pan.
- Let it cook on high heat for at least 3 minutes before you turn it over, using a spatula.
- Keep turning until it's brown. If you would like to shallow-fry, you can drizzle a few drops of oil and fry, otherwise just take it off and eat it with ghee/butter.

Makki roti and saag is often served with plain yoghurt, mango pickle and fresh green chillis. In Punjab, where winters are harsh, people sit around the open woodfire stove on the verandah and the whole family is served the fresh rotis straight from the stove. While we might not have an open woodfire stove, my mum still continues this tradition of serving rotis while they're hot.

Where is the Dal?

My tribute to a classic Black Eyed Peas song

If you have love for your family
You will always have atta in the pantry
And from that atta you can cook roti
Take it for lunch so you don't get hungry

Hanger is what you don't wanna demonstrate.
That's exactly how anger works and operates.
Gotta add masala just to set it straight.
Take control of your kitchen and mate
let your tummy gravitate
to the dal y'all

(Bridge)
Mango pickle and mint chutney
Are condiments for dahl makhani
Can you taste the hot chillies?
Better add some more veggies
Papa, Papa, Papa, loves it
Garnished with coriander
My tummy's got me, got me questionin'

(Chorus)
Where is the dal?
Where is the dal?
Where is the dal?
Where is the dal? The dal. The dal.

Yellow Dal

This is the basic bitch of all Indian food. When I was younger, I hated dal. It was boring and repetitive, but now it's my favourite. I love cooking this when I can't think of anything for dinner because it doesn't take long to cook and can be served with fun snacks like pappadums or crunchy potato crisps.

Serves 2–3

Ingredients
1 cup dry red lentils
3 cups water
½ tsp turmeric powder
1 tsp salt
1 green chilli
2 tbsp ghee
1 tsp cumin seeds
½ tsp coriander powder
½ tsp cumin powder
handful of fresh coriander

Method

- Soak the lentils for 1–2 hours (but you can skip this step and the world won't end)
- Drain the water and add fresh water
- Boil the water and lentils with turmeric, salt and chilli with the lid open until it starts bubbling
- Cover the pot and simmer on low heat for at least 30 mins, stirring well
- Keep checking until it reaches a smooth consistency. You don't want the lentils separated from the water – it should be soupy
- If you have a dal disaster, which I have had plenty of, use a whisk to smooth out the dal
- In a small saucepan, heat up the ghee and add cumin seeds
- Pour this mixture onto the dal
- Add the coriander powder and cumin powder
- Garnish with fresh coriander

While cooking, you're welcome to sing 'Where is the Dal' – it makes the food taste better. Trust me.

Pull for an Arts Degree

The University of Western Australia has an engineering block
And in that engineering block are some male toilets
And in those male toilets there is a toilet paper dispenser.
And above the toilet paper dispenser is an arrow pointing down
At the reel coming through
Where a student has inscribed:
'Pull for an Arts Degree'.

PULL FOR AN ARTS DEGREE!?

While imagining people wiping their arses on my degree,
I think back to Year 3
When my teacher told me:
'Every child is a different kind of flower
And together you make this world a beautiful garden.'
Well, I beg your pardon,
Engineering boy,
For destroying
A little part of me, the heart in me,
The faith in me, don't hate on me,
Stop demeaning me
And the worth of my degree.

You might be one of them:
Measuring success by those dollar dollar bills
Superior in your exterior
As if you shit a different way to the rest of us

Just stop for a minute and chill
Everybody look to the left
Everybody look to the right
Art is all around us, within us
So why you tryna kill

The free thinkers
Creatives
Innovators
Debaters
Communicators

Those buildings behind
The selfies on your backpacking trips
Might have been built by engineers and labourers
But were rediscovered by historians and archaeologists
With Arts degrees.

As a young woman
In this country
In today's century
I am grateful
To have received
An education.

My commiserations to the women of the world who are denied this right.

My own mother
'The other'
Was brought up in another land.
In a time where the sublime nursery rhyme
Abandoned education for a wedding band.

Like many of us in Oz,
My parents saved those rupees just coz
I could get a degree.
Whatever degree that may be.

So save the worrying about employability, for me
No, it's not a waste of money
And I don't want fries with that honey

Let's go through the diamond window
Where you might be able to follow
That life
Is more than the rules some of us have created
And they CAN be changed.

It's what you do with that HECS debt that truly counts.

Graduates, don't apologise for your BA
Just because people don't for their BS.
You is kind. You is smart. You is important.

Bringing Home the Besan

I think I got my entrepreneurial spirit from my dad.

Before I was born, Papa mostly worked in banks, but he had also been convinced by a series of sales folk to buy a restaurant, then a dairy shop, a garment business and so on. This was during the start of the recession in the early '90s. When my family moved to Perth in 1992, unemployment was at 11 per cent and Dad felt it firsthand. He applied for 150 jobs and was unsuccessful in getting any of them. For the first time, Mum headed out into the workforce. Did a childcare course and worked as a childcare worker, then did a commercial chef course and worked at restaurants. Dad was now a freelance accountant and earning a similar amount to Mum. So, with some help from Centrelink, they managed to pay for rent, bills, food. Things weren't that bad and they started their own catering business from home in 2002.

Some of the catering gigs were at Indian classical music concerts, so I was exposed to arts and culture from a young age. But it was never labelled as 'the arts' – just something we did on the weekend. Since I was four years old, I wrote and directed plays for Mothers' Day, Fathers' Day and birthdays.

I didn't have my own room till I was in Year 10, but what kept me going all those years was dreaming of one day having a bedroom that had red velvet curtains and a stage like on Broadway. I don't know where I got this image from, but it stuck.

Maybe I went to a Spare Parts Puppet show with my mum because we'd won some tickets in a newspaper contest. My sister loved entering those. But the first play I remember experiencing was brought to Leeming Senior High School by Barking Gecko in 2009. It was called *Hoods* and starred Andrea Gibbs and Sam Longley. Two people I never dreamt I would be working with fifteen years later.

I initially tried to be like the men in my family by studying physics and chem and getting my manual licence, but I failed so I swapped to English lit, drama and automatic driving.

My parents weren't the type to force me to do anything. I almost wish they were stereotypes who had encouraged me to be a doctor. Instead, they told me to choose whatever profession I wanted as long as I worked hard, managed my ego and treated everyone equally. Although maybe they wouldn't have given me the same advice if I'd told them I wanted to be an artist or a performer.

In 2013, I got into a leadership course in Prague. I did a PowerPoint presentation to convince my dad to let me go, saying I'd get a scholarship to pay for most of it and my Jeanswest job at the Kwinana Hub would cover the rest. In Prague, a peer told me to look up spoken word poetry and I became inspired to try it out. I ended up performing in a national competition at the Sydney Opera House, and that was the first time I met artists working full-time as artists. Poets touring the world with their books.

Most kids tell their parents what their career choice is over dinner or a phone call, but not me. I decided to go on national television to show them who I wanted to be.

I still remember the night my audition for *Australia's Got Talent* aired. It was 2016 and I was living in Melbourne and my parents rang me and told me that their landline hadn't stopped ringing all night. Then all week. All month! Everyone they knew from Bahrain to New Zealand to Pakistan to the local Gurdwara saw me on a crappy WhatsApp recording someone had taken of the TV. Twenty million people saw that crappy WhatsApp recording. I didn't even know what 'viral' was or what would happen next. And not to sound dramatic but my life kinda changed. I was still the same Sukhjit but more people knew what I was doing and what I wanted to say. I was in a privileged position of having a platform to speak my truth.

From that moment onwards, it became my mission for the next few years to prove to Sikh families all over the world that their kids can pursue the arts. That being an artist was a respectable and sustainable career choice. My whole childhood, I saw how underrepresented we were in the media and it drove my ambition.

Over the last decade, I have had the privilege of doing twenty-six film gigs and eight theatre gigs, facilitating thirty-five workshop series, MCing forty-five events, sitting on thirty-eight panels, appearing on Australian and international TV eight times, exhibiting work at six exhibitions, participating in eight labs, releasing a song, judging eight sets of awards, producing fourteen works, speaking to twenty-five schools, featuring in seven podcasts, having ten pieces of writing published, and performing poetry at 145 gigs all as an independent artist. And when I was eighteen, I got to be the Minister for Culture and the Arts for five days during Youth Parliament. If I wasn't such a crier, I would probably pursue that goal as well!

Many generous people have taken a chance on me along the way, even when I hadn't done that job or gig before. I've learnt a lot by doing. I've taken heaps of risks that ended up paying off. From a young age, I learnt how to advocate for myself and put myself out there to seek opportunities to further my development. I never waited around for phone calls; I had to be proactive and hustle.

Also, I had two amazing teachers – Mr Wheatley in primary school and Miss Lacy in high school – who supported me and believed in me. That's where it all truly began.

Although representation is better than what it was in the '90s, I am hearing so many stories from all over Australia of underrepresented artists leaving the industry because the industry didn't do its absolute best to create a culturally safe environment.

As I head into my next decade as an artist, I want to make change happen faster than its current pace. And, as my parents would add, continue to be someone who works hard and manages their ego.

Collectables

Yeah, you're the token, an Aussie slogan
Fresh off the boat or a proud bogan
You're the slum dog, they're your saviour
You're the complex of White Australia
You're the mentee not the mentor
The advisor not the director
You're the IT guy or the Uber ride

Would you like a serve of pickled veg or rice on the side?
Would you like a serve of pickled veg or rice on the side?
Would you like a serve of pickled veg or rice on the side?
Would you like a serve of pickled veg or rice on the side?

You're the trauma porn on Struggle Street
Your time to shine is in Harmony Week
You're hospitable, humble, grateful and kind
Your fair go is coming, just give it more time

You're the collectable
When you collect that dust
You'll be replaceable
Cos it's not too much
To find another new recruit
That comes ticking the boxes
It's diversity (diversity)

Not your collectable
Educate yourself
Not your collectable
Get me off your shelf
Not your collectable
You really need some help
Not just another trophy here to help collect your wealth

Not your collectable
Educate yourself
Not your collectable
You really need some help
Not your collectable
Educate yourself
You really need some help
Get me off your shelf

Way too hairy for *The Bachelor*
You're SBS, you're the educator
You're the panellist on *Q&A*
Too caramel for *Woman's Day*
Too controversial for the commercial
The comedian, a chameleon
You're one of the good...
If you're not in Australia then where the bloody hell are ya?
If you don't assimilate then who the bloody hell are ya?

Ao challo hun kariye, iss da upaa
Tussin bollo, dil kholo, kardo kamaal
Tell 'em roop mera, seva meri, karo p-chhaann
Naal kharre, assin larre, assin desh di haan jaan
Mill ke banayiye, hun nava samaaj
Insaf de naal, sab hojaange azaad
Insaf de naal, sab hojaange azaad
Insaf de naal, sab hojaange azaad

TRANSLATION:
Come let's sort out a solution
Speak, open your heart and do something amazing
Recognise my appearance and my service
Tell 'em: together we stood, together we fought, we are the lifeforce of this country
Let's build a new society together
With fairness/justice we will all become free

Not your collectable
Educate yourself
Not your collectable
You really need some help
Not your collectable
Educate yourself
You really need some help
Get me off your shelf

Not your collectable
Educate yourself
Not your collectable
You really need some help
Not your collectable
Educate yourself
You really need some help
Get me off your shelf

If you feel like I'm joking, then check yourself
'Cos I don't wanna be just another up on your shelf
And if this sounds like you, then protect yourself
Recognise identities, enrich societies
With fairness and justice
We WILL achieve equality

Dinnertime Conversations

I remember being quite an inquisitive young girl when it came to asking my parents about life's big questions. Growing up with a spiritually wise Papa and my unfiltered curiosity was the perfect recipe to make dinnertime conversations very deep.

I would often ask what Waheguru Ji, the Eternal Force or 'God', looked like. Smelt like. Felt like. This was when Papa would get me to draw what I thought Waheguru Ji looked like.

Surprisingly, my decolonised imagination didn't draw an old white man in some clouds. Instead, I have a vague memory of drawing a glowing yellow light in the middle of the page with rainbows spewing out.

Papa then said, 'See that light you've drawn, Sukhjit – that's what happens when you merge with Waheguru Ji.'

'How will I know that I've merged with Waheguru Ji? Will someone tell me?' asked my innocence.

'No no, when it happens it will happen so fast you won't even know. Life can be taken away from you very quickly and very easily, with Waheguru Ji's will.'

'How do you merge with Waheguru Ji?' I asked.

Papa replied, 'By removing your ego.'

'I don't want to merge with Waheguru Ji,' I said. 'It sounds scary. I have so much I want to do in life.'

'A Sikh does not fear death, Sukhjit. Your soul and spirit never die. Only your body. In Gurbani, our Sikh scriptures, this temporary body is compared to the five elements of the universe. Wind. Water. Fire. Space. Earth. These elements are within you and when your body is cremated, it merges with the universe.'

He recited a verse from our scriptures, which loosely translated to:

> The wind merges into the wind.
> The light blends into the light.
> The dust becomes one with the dust . . .
> Mortal beings are bound by the bonds of doubt and attachment.
> No one dies; no one is capable of dying.
> The soul does not perish; it is imperishable.

As a thirty-year-old, I don't necessarily fear my own death, but I fear people dying around me. But I don't spend that much time deeply thinking about my relationship to spirituality anymore. I've forgotten how to ponder life's big questions. Maybe I've succumbed to the material world, possessed by capitalism and all its sickly fruits. Maybe I've become too attached to humans and place and my body. Maybe my ego hasn't been checked. Maybe I won't merge with Waheguru Ji after all.

I've spent the last decade evolving into the Sikh I want to be – but is that strong spiritual soul still in me?

Can I still get lost in gems of Gurbani?

Do I still practise the religious rituals?

Do I believe Waheguru Ji exists?

Which part of me is Sikh?

The part that puts on a phulkari?

The part that gives a shit about humanity?

It was such a big part of my childhood – weekends, schooling, family life, friendships – then later became a massive part of my career, my writing, my inspiration, my identity . . .

As I look out to the next decade of growth, I wonder what will be:

Will I be different?

Will I be faithful?

Will I be Fully Sikh?

Kulfi

Kulfi is the highlight of summer in Northern India, but now communities all over the world have added their own flavours: mango, pistachio, almond, saffron, rosewater . . . The list goes on! But I'm a vanilla girl and by vanilla, I mean the original kulfi.

Makes 18–20 in aluminium kulfi moulds

Ingredients
600 ml whipped cream
340 ml can evaporated milk
385 ml can sweetened condensed milk
½ cup almond meal or almond powder
2 cardamoms, crushed

Method

- Mix everything together then pour the mixture into kulfi moulds or small containers to freeze. They take around 8 hours to set before you can serve them.

When I performed my play *Fully Sikh* at the State Theatre Centre in Perth, the gelato place next door called Chicho Gelato made this recipe for opening night. It was a very special moment to have a local business honour a recipe from Punjab in Perth.

Acknowledgements

Perun – my oak, my bestie, my beloved

Papa and Mumsie – the two most generous humans I know

Harjit, Manjit and Gurkiran – the three of the funniest and fun-est humans I know

Daniel Connell – my artistic sounding-board

Terri-ann White and Rebecca Bauert – for making my dream a reality

The recipes in this book involve my own improvisations in the kitchen. They are not precise in measurement and methodology, but are just like my mother taught me. They provide an introduction to third culture cooking.

Publication Details

'Gurdwara Day' was first published in *Growing Up Indian in Australia*, published by Black Inc. in 2024.

'Winner of Peace' was originally published as 'The Lionness' in *Tongues Magazine* in 2018.

'Pardēs' was commissioned for Melville Storylines 2022.

'Kush Dil' was commissioned for Red Room Poetry (NSW) August 2023.

'Monga Khan and the Humble Hansons' was originally published in *The Legend of Monga Khan*, edited by Royce Kurmelovs, in 2016.

'Collectables' is available to stream at https://sukhjit.bandcamp.com/track/collectables

About Upswell

Upswell Publishing was established in 2021 by Terri-ann White as a not-for-profit press. A perceived gap in the market for distinctive literary works in fiction, poetry and narrative non-fiction was the motivation. In her years as a bookseller, writer and then publisher, Terri-ann has maintained a watch on literary books and the way they insinuate themselves into a cultural space and are then located within our literary and cultural inheritance. She is interested in making books to last: books with the potential to still be noticed, and noted, after decades and thus be ripe to influence new literary histories.

The Foundation for Australian Literary Studies (FALS) has supported the author as the recipient of the first PF Rowland Manuscript Development Grant. In partnership with the Publisher, this Grant supports an emerging writer financially, allowing her to work with Terri-ann White and Upswell Publishing, to complete a manuscript.

Associate Professor Roger Osborne, FALS Executive Director, describes the Grant as part of the Foundation's dedication to celebrating Australian writers and writing for more than 56 years.

The Grant is made possible by the P. F. Rowland Memorial Fund. More information on Percy Fritz Rowland can be accessed here.

About this typeface

Book designer Becky Chilcott chose Foundry Origin not only as a strong, carefully considered, and dependable typeface, but also to honour her late friend and mentor, type designer Freda Sack, who oversaw the project. Designed by Freda's long-standing colleague, Stuart de Rozario, much like Upswell Publishing, Foundry Origin was created out of the desire to say something new.